Home Cell Group Explosion

Home Cell Group Explosion:

How Your Small Group Can Grow and Multiply

by Joel Comiskey

TOUCH PUBLICATIONS
P.O. Box 19888 • Houston, TX 77224-9888

International Standard Book Number: 1-880828-06-5

Editing, book layout, cover design and illustration: Elizabeth Bruns, Rick Chandler, Jim Egli, Randall Neighbour, and Brian Williams.

TOUCH Publications is the book-publishing division of TOUCH Outreach Ministries, a resource and consulting ministry for churches with a vision for cell-based local church structure.

Available from:
TOUCH Outreach Ministries
P.O. Box 19888 • Houston, TX 77224-9888, USA
Telephone (281) 497-7901 • Fax (281) 497-0904
Website: www.touchusa.org

CONTENTS

FOREWORD

T his is a book for the harvest.

We are now living in the midst of the greatest harvest of souls that Christian history has ever recorded. More people are being born again and more churches are being multiplied than anyone could have imagined only a few years ago.

That's the good news. The bad news is that much of the fruit being harvested is not fruit that remains. While we rightly rejoice over the current expansion of the kingdom of God, those in the know realize that it should be expanding even more than it actually is.

Why is it, for example, that city-wide evangelistic campaigns, which continue to be popular decade after decade, find so few of their converts in local churches one year later? The norm has been that of those individuals who make first-time decisions for Christ at the campaign, the number who end up in local churches runs between 3 percent and 16 percent. No one I know, including the evangelists themselves, is happy with those figures.

Moreover, many churches that have strong evangelistic ministries and that do see considerable numbers of new converts coming into their churches also have wide open back doors. The annual growth of their church does not reflect the inflow of new members as it should.

The situations I have just described are familiar enough, and they are widespread. However, all evangelistic efforts and all growing churches have not been victims of people falling through the cracks. By and large, the churches which are retaining the greatest percentage of the harvest are those churches which have successfully developed their infrastructure. There are different ways of dealing with that infrastructure, but the majority of the churches which have done it today and which have broken growth barrier after growth barrier are churches which have stressed home cell groups.

No one knows that better than my friend Joel Comiskey. He is a combination of a local church practitioner and a painstaking scholar. Instead of writing a book on "here is how we do it in our church," Joel spent hundreds of hours and thousands of dollars to visit personally eight of the highest-visibility cell group churches today, to interview their leaders, to participate in the life of the churches, and to record his findings in this book, *Home Cell Group Explosion*.

I love this book because it is not focused on the home cell, but on the lost. Other books deal with the dynamics of the cell itself, but this one focuses on the multiplication of cells for the greatest evangelistic results. If your church has an open back door, you have in your hands a guidebook to close it. If some of the fruit you are seeing is not fruit that remains, here is how to change the situation for good.

Home Cell Group Explosion is truly a book for the harvest!

C. Peter Wagner
Fuller Theological Seminary

PREFACE

As I write, several dozen books on small groups are lined up before me. They cover topics from the Bible and small groups, to small-group dynamics, to pure cell church ministry. Not one of them, however, focuses on how small groups evangelize. Dr. Van Engen, professor of Missiology at Fuller Theological Seminary, expressed this void during my Ph.D. proposal defense. "There are enough books on small-group dynamics," he said. "However, we need to learn how small groups evangelize." That day I felt commissioned. He gave me a new objective for my research. This, then, is a book about how small groups evangelize, grow and eventually multiply.

INTRODUCTION

Ever so subtly, God has led me down the path of small-group ministry. Three years after receiving Jesus Christ at age 17, I felt called to start a home Bible study. Friends gathered each week to hear this young, zealous teenager; by God's grace, some of them stayed. During one of those sessions, Jesus called me to be a missionary.

As a missionary candidate with the Christian and Missionary Alliance, I planted an inner-city church in Long Beach, California. To start the church in 1984, I gathered people in my home. That same year, David Yonggi Cho, pastor of the world's largest church, presented lectures on church growth at Fuller Theological Seminary. I sat awed as he related story after story about how every one of the 500,000 members of Yoido Full Gospel Church in Seoul, Korea, received pastoral care through one of the church's 20,000 cell groups.

Filled with enthusiasm, I bought Cho's book *Successful Home Cell Groups* and began to teach key leaders in my church.[1] The excitement lasted for awhile, and we started four cells. But after we introduced a Sunday morning service, I lost the grip on my small-group focus. Church chores sapped my strength. Still, I never lost the vision and excitement for what a church could become through a small-group ministry.

A few years later, I was a missionary in Ecuador, and the opportunity arrived to reclaim the embers of my vision for small-group ministry. My wife and I, placed on a pastoral team in a strategic church in Quito, Ecuador, were supposed to stimulate growth that would result in a daughter church. Many received Christ month after month, but relatively few stayed. We wrestled as a pastoral team about how to close "the back door." We planned Sunday school activities, new believers' classes and visitation programs, all with little success.

My first year on that pastoral team was a dark night of the soul. The other pastors listened politely as I made suggestions in broken Spanish. I longed to communicate church growth ideas, but I lacked the fluency and cultural knowledge. Week after week, I left the pastoral team meeting discouraged and downtrodden. At one point, the team leader seriously considered replacing me with a more experienced missionary who was returning from furlough.

In those dark moments, as I hovered between success and failure as a first-term missionary, God began to speak. He showed me that our church (El Batán) desperately needed a cell ministry. God placed a burden on my heart that I couldn't shake. I knew it was of Him. Insights from David Yonggi Cho flooded my mind. When I shared this vision with the pastoral team, they gave my wife and me the green light to pursue it.

We already were working with university students, so we organized them into five groups that focused on evangelism and discipleship. Those groups began to grow. Soon the young married couples wanted us to organize small groups among them. Those groups began to multiply and bear fruit, too. We grew from the initial five groups in 1992 to 51 groups in 1994. About 400 people, most of them new converts, were added to the El Batán Church and began to attend the Sunday morning services. In Ecuador, where only 3.5 percent of the population knew Jesus Christ as their Lord and Savior, it was especially clear that this was a work of God.

We eventually birthed a daughter church from El Batán. Using the cell concept, we started with 10 cell groups and 150 people. In less than one year, the 10 cells multiplied to 20 and the church grew to 350 people. The church growth continues unabated with the cells as its base.

God is sovereign. Never in my wildest dreams could I have imagined traveling around the world "in search of the perfect cell church." But that's exactly what I did for two years. My Ph.D. studies on unlocking the secrets of the cell movement took me to Korea, Singapore, Louisiana, El Salvador, Honduras, Colombia,

Ecuador and Peru. My mentor, C. Peter Wagner, believed in me and my work, thus providing needed inspiration.

I know what it's like to start a cell ministry from scratch. I've experienced failure, but I've also tasted success. From both personal experience and thorough research, I've discovered dynamic principles and practical insights to share with others who have a vision for reaching the world through cell churches. By God's grace, they are presented in the following pages.

1

SUCCESSFUL
CELL-BASED CHURCHES

"If you want to know how churches grow, study growing churches!" This one sentence embodies the core of church growth research. You may have thought this was a book about small-group evangelism, but the two can't be separated. At least they shouldn't. Small-group evangelism and dynamic church growth are two sides of the same coin. They are one.

When I began to study small-group evangelism, I chose to research the most prominent and fastest growing cell-based churches in the world. Why not study what works? These churches are located in eight different countries and four distinct cultures.

As the table at the top of the following page illustrates, small-group evangelism that results in dynamic church growth is a worldwide phenomenon. No longer is the U.S. the fountain of Christian knowledge for the rest of the world. However, one excellent example in the U.S. is Bethany World Prayer Center in Baker, Louisiana, the premier cell church in the U.S. Each year, 1,000 pastors attend small-group seminars at BWPC. Bethany is on the cutting edge primarily because of its willingness to learn from other fast-growing churches around the world. Bethany has sent its leaders to capture principles from cell churches in Colombia, El Salvador, Korea and Singapore.

To learn from the eight case-study churches, I spent an average of eight days in each one. More than 700 cell leaders completed my 29-question survey, designed to determine why some cell leaders succeed and others fail at evangelizing and giving birth to a new cell group.[1] The questionnaire explored such areas as the cell

Abbreviation	Name of Church	Location	Senior Pastor	No. of Cells	No. of Worshippers
BWPC	Bethany World Prayer Center	Baker, LA USA	Larry Stockstill	600	8,000
CCG	The Christian Center of Guayaquil	Guayaquil, Ecuador	Jerry Smith	2,000	7,000
EC	Elim Church	San Salvador, El Salvador	Mario Vega	5,500	35,000
FCBC	Faith Community Baptist Church	Singapore	Lawrence Khong	600	10,000
ICM	The International Charismatic Mission	Bogota, Colombia	César Castellanos	20,000	47,000
LAC	Love Alive Church	Tegucigalpa, Honduras	René Peñalba	1,000	7,000
LWC	Living Water Church	Lima, Peru	Peter Hornung Bobbio	900	9,000
YFGC	Yoido Full Gospel Church	Seoul, Korea	David Cho	25,000	253,000[2]

Table 1. Description of Case-Study Churches

leader's training, social status, devotions, education, preparation of material, age, spiritual gifts, gender, etc. This statistical analysis helped keep my bias at bay and enabled me to unlock common principles across diverse cultures.

Donald McGavran once gave an illustration of two pastors who preached the Word of God. One claimed that his church grew because he preached the Word of God, while the other insisted that his church did not grow because he preached the Word of God. I chuckled at first, but then acknowledged its application to the current scene. So often, Christian leaders really don't know why churches grow or decline. Individual interpretations and opinions prevail. Similar confusion abounds about cell multiplication.

As the population continues to explode in the 21st century, the cell church model holds exciting possibilities of reaching a lost world for Jesus Christ. I pray that the information gathered from these cell-based churches will help you and your church more effectively complete the mission of our Lord Jesus Christ.

2

CELL CHURCH
BASICS

DEFINING "CELL CHURCH"

So what exactly is a cell church? In everyday terminology, it's simply a church that has placed evangelistic small groups at the core of its ministry. Cell ministry is not "another program"; it's the very heart of the church. As Lawrence Khong, pastor of Faith Community Baptist Church in Singapore, says:

> There is a vast difference between a church with cells and a cell church. ... We don't do anything else except the cell. All the things the church must do—training, equipping, discipleship, evangelism, prayer, worship—are done through the cell. Our Sunday service is just the corporate celebration.[1]

Cells are open, evangelism-focused small groups that are entwined into the life of the church. They meet weekly to build up each other as members of the Body of Christ, and to spread the gospel to those who don't know Jesus. The ultimate goal of each cell is to multiply itself as the group grows through evangelism and then conversions. This is how new members are added to the church and to the kingdom of God. Members of cell groups also are encouraged to attend the celebration service of the entire church, where cells come together for worship.

This foundational link between a church community and its small groups is one of the significant differences between cell churches and house churches. Ralph Neighbour Jr. makes a helpful clarification:

There is a distinct difference between the house church and the cell group movements. House Churches tend to collect a community of 15-25 people who meet together on a weekly basis. Usually, each House Church stands alone. While they may be in touch with nearby House Churches, they usually do not recognize any further structure beyond themselves.[2]

Again, not all small groups are cell groups. Experts estimate that in the U.S. alone, 80 million adults belong to a small group.[3] One out of six of those are new members of a small group, which shows that small groups are alive and growing.[4] Lyle Schaller, after listing 20 innovations in the modern U.S. church scene, notes: ". . . Perhaps most important of all, [is] the decision by tens of millions of teenagers and adults to place a high personal priority on weekly participation in serious, in-depth, lay-led, and continuing Bible study and prayer groups."[5]

Much of the small-group movement in the United States, however, promotes personal health at the expense of evangelistic outreach. For example, Michael Mack in *The Synergy Church* analyzes the "covenant model" of U.S. small groups: ". . . New people are not invited or welcomed—whether the group at first intended for it to be closed or not. There is no organized system for multiplication of these groups."[6] Mack goes on to say, ". . . in many churches small groups are not open to newcomers and are not set up to reproduce themselves."[7]

Such a mind-set is unthinkable in a cell church. Evangelism that leads to cell multiplication fuels the rest of the church. Dale Galloway, founder of New Hope Community Church in Portland, Oregon, declares, "Closed groups are restricted and dead-end, and they do not fulfill the Great Commission."[8] Carl F. George is even more emphatic:

Show me a nurturing group not regularly open to new life, and I will guarantee that it's dying. If cells are units of redemption, then no one can button up the lifeboats and hang out a sign, 'You can't come in here.' The notion of group members shutting themselves off in order to accomplish discipleship is a scourge that will destroy any church's missionary mandate.[9]

Cell ministry is the very backbone of the eight churches included in this case study. They organize pastoral staff, membership, baptisms, offerings, and celebration services around cell ministry. Everyone in the church is encouraged to attend a cell. For example, statistics at Love Alive Church in Tegucigalpa, Honduras, show that 90 percent of the 7,500 weekend worshippers participate in a weekly cell group. Not all the churches in this case study experience such high a percentage of cell participation, but each church stresses the importance of cell membership.

WHY "CELL"?

Cells, biologically, are "the smallest structural unit of an organism that is capable of independent functioning."[10] One drop of blood, for instance, has about 300 million red cells! Just as individual cells join to form the body of a human being, cells in a church form the Body of Christ. Further, each biological cell grows and reproduces its parts until it divides into two cells. The total genetic package received in part from the parent is re-established in each daughter cell.[11] This also occurs in healthy church cells. As we will see in later chapters, mother-daughter cell multiplication aspires to reproduce the "total genetic package" into the new group.

GRASPING THE PROCESS

Just as human cells pass through specific stages, so should small groups. The chart at the top of the following page depicts those stages: (Chart courtesy of Bethany World Prayer Center)

LEARNING STAGE

Initially, each human cell resembles a blob of protoplasm. Individual parts are almost indistinguishable. Although the cell possesses the genetic code for multiplication, it must grow and develop first. Small groups follow a similar pattern. Members initially gaze at each other with an unknowing expectancy, and the first stage of cell-group life is characterized by the members

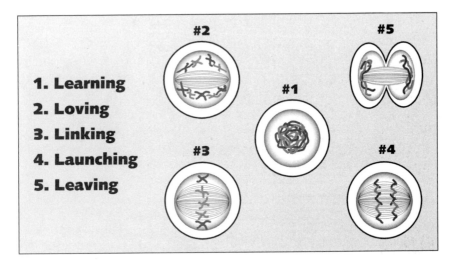

Figure 1. The Process of Cell Multiplication

getting to know each other. Perhaps cell leaders should emphasize ice-breaker ("get to know each other") skills during the early days. The learning stage lasts about one month.

LOVING STAGE

The chromosomes in a human cell eventually begin to pair, although not in a straight line. In a similar fashion, cell members take their masks off during the loving stage. People see each other for who they really are. Conflict often develops when someone forgets to bring the refreshments or arrives late. Hence, some call this "the conflict stage." The loving stage also lasts approximately one month.

LINKING STAGE

In a human cell, the once free-floating chromosomes suddenly begin to form a line at mid-cell. At a cell group's midpoint—somewhere around the third or fourth month—the members begin to find their roles. For example, everyone begins to acknowledge Judy's talent with worship or John's gift for counseling. This is a good time for cell evangelism training. This stage lasts about one month.

LAUNCHING STAGE

The chromosome strands begin to line up in east-west positions, getting ready to launch and make an exact duplicate of itself. At this point in the small group, members focus on evangelism. Although the cell always reaches out, the launching time highlights group evangelism as the primary activity. The launching stage occurs from the fourth month until the cell multiplies.

LEAVING STAGE

As the one cell prepares to give birth to an identical cell, the chromosomes separate and eventually divide (multiply). In a small group, new leaders are raised up and trained to lead a cell even as new members join. When the group is large enough, multiplication occurs. The leaving stage might last up to one year.

Not every group multiplies, but there is the danger of stagnation when one doesn't. Larry Stockstill, head pastor of Bethany World Prayer Center, jokingly noted at a 1996 cell conference at BWPC, "Usually, a group that only has four people sitting around looking at each other after one year are quite happy to get out of there!"

SETTING THE GOAL: MULTIPLICATION

The heart of cell-based ministry is evangelism, and the eight most prominent cell churches in the world position their cell ministry primarily to evangelize lost men and women. These churches accept Jesus' Great Commission (Matthew 28:18-20) as their marching order. They advance into the enemy's camp of non-Christians and even track their "progress." Church leaders set quantifiable goals for their cell ministry, and some even promote "healthy competition" among cell leadership. Passion for the lost is the motivation that keeps everything in perspective. Far more effective than "one-on-one" evangelism, the cells in these churches function like nets that spread out over entire cities. Buses haul the catch to the celebration service for worship.

Mikell Neuman, professor at Western Seminary in Portland, Oregon, confirms these findings with his recent research. He makes these observations about small-group characteristics that transcend culture:

"While we suspected evangelism was a key to home group ministries, we were surprised at the force of its importance. The churches in this study do not divide the ministry into the lost and the saved with special home groups for each. In any given group, one might find a mix of non-Christians, new Christians, and more mature Christians. People come to know Christ in the home group with their friends or family who are already Christians, and in the same group they grow in maturity."[12]

As founding pastor of DOVE Christian Fellowship in Pennsylvania, Larry Kreider understands the dynamics of cell ministry so well that his church, which he started from scratch, now plants daughter churches worldwide. Kreider believes that, "The main purpose for every cell group must be to run a rescue shop within a yard of hell. Otherwise, the cell becomes a social club without any power."[13] Ralph Neighbour Jr. writes in *Where Do We Go From Here?*, "This common vision—reaching the lost and equipping believers for that task—provides the healthy continuity between all the cell groups."[14]

Clearly, evangelism that results in the proliferation of cell groups is the most distinguishing feature of the cell church worldwide. My case study reveals that more than 60 percent of the 700 cell leaders surveyed had multiplied their group at least once, and that it took about nine months to do so. These leaders know that evangelism must lead to multiplication, and that small-group evangelism is never an end in itself. Furthermore, church growth is the ultimate fruit of cell multiplication. Not all cell churches have the same level of success in pulling in the net. But the goal and vision are the same.

UNDERSTANDING EVANGELISM'S HISTORY

Solomon declared that nothing new exists under the sun, and

small-group evangelism is no exception. It has played an important role since Jesus formed His church and rapid multiplication of first-century house churches spread the flame of God's love throughout the world. *Home Cell Groups and House Churches* notes:

> *"Another significant matter about evangelism in the New Testament is that much of it—if not most of the more enduring type—took place in the house churches. This was true not simply because the larger homes were able to accommodate the function. It was also true because proclamation took place as a result of the total witness of the interrelated functions of church life in the homes."*[15]

But since the early church, small-group ministry has focused primarily on Christian edification and spiritual growth. There were exceptions, such as the monastic bands and the Moravian missionary teams who spread the gospel message through small groups. But not until John Wesley and Methodism did we again catch a glimpse of the potential for small-group evangelism.

EVANGELISM IN EARLY METHODISM

John Wesley was the pioneer of small-group evangelism. By the end of the 18th century, Wesley had developed more than 10,000 cells groups (called classes).[16] Hundreds of thousands of people participated in his small-group system.[17]

Wesley wasn't persuaded that someone had made a decision for Christ until that person became involved in a small group. Wesley was more interested in discipleship than in a decision. The classes served as an evangelistic tool (most conversions occurred in this context) and as a discipling agent.[18] George G. Hunter III writes, "To Wesley, evangelism . . . took place primarily in the class meetings and in people's hearts in the hours following the class meetings.[19] Wesley acknowledged that the beginnings of a person's faith could be incubated more effectively in a warm Christian environment than in the chill of the world.[20]

As the forerunner of the modern cell movement, Wesley promoted evangelism that led to rapid multiplication. Hunter notes, "He was driven to multiplying 'classes' for these served best as recruiting groups, as ports of entry for new people, and for involving awakened people with the gospel and power."[21] Wesley would preach and then invite the people to join a class. Apparently, they multiplied primarily as a result of planting new classes, much like the emphasis on cell planting today.[22] The primary objective in his preaching was starting new classes.[23] T.A. Hegre notes,

> *I believe that the success of Wesley was due to his habit of establishing small groups. His converts would meet regularly in groups of about a dozen people. If the group became too large, it would divide, and it might continue to divide again and again.*[24]

Small-group ministry constantly faces a dilemma: maintaining the intimacy of a small group while fulfilling Christ's command to evangelize. Cell multiplication is the only proven way to remain small while faithfully reaching out. Wesley practiced this principle and laid the foundation for the modern cell-church explosion.

DAVID YONGGI CHO AND THE MODERN CELL MOVEMENT

If Wesley was the forerunner of the small-group movement, David Yonggi Cho ushered in the new era. Cho is the founding pastor of Yoido Full Gospel Church in Seoul, Korea, the largest church in the world.

This church has grown to 25,000 cells, and the seven Sunday services draw approximately 253,000 worshippers each week. About 25,000 attend the 6 a.m. service. The church is still packing in the faithful for the 3 p.m. service, and all six basement chapels (with closed-circuit television) are overflowing.

Cho credits the growth of his church to the cell-group system.[25] He commissions each cell to bring non-Christians to Jesus Christ, with the goal of multiplying the cell. If the cell leaders fail to reach their goals, Cho sends them to the church's Prayer Mountain retreat to fast and pray.

Since Cho initiated his cell ministry in the early 1970s, many other pastors have followed his lead. Yoido Full Gospel Church has directly or indirectly influenced every cell church in the world today. For example, the pastors of the two largest and most influential cell churches in Latin America—César Castellanos of the International Charismatic Mission in Bogota, Colombia, and Sergio Solórzano of La Misión Cristiana Elim in San Salvador, El Salvador—visited Cho's church before launching their own cell ministries.

Pastor César Castellano's visit to Yoido in 1986 revolutionized the small-group ministry at the International Charismatic Mission. Through an awesome move of God's Spirit, the 10,000+ cell groups are penetrating every corner of Bogota. At the front of the church's sanctuary, huge banners declare the focus: "The goal of our church: 30,000 cell groups by December 31, 1997!" With such rapid growth, this church soon may surpass the number of cell groups at Yoido.

Likewise, Pastor Sergio Solórzano visited Cho's church in 1985 before initiating his cell ministry. By October 1996, 116,000 people were attending 5,300 cell groups. This church's incredible commitment to reach the masses is seen each Sunday as more than 600 city buses, rented by the cell groups, transport cell members to the celebration services. Also amazing is how every person who attends a Sunday service is counted and entered into the computer by Monday morning.

David Cho's influence cannot be overestimated. C. Kirk Hadaway makes this comment:

> The word spread that Paul [before he changed his name to David] Cho's church and several other huge churches in Seoul reached their massive size through home cell groups and that the technique will work anywhere. A movement began, and pastors have flocked to Korea to learn. . . . Churches all over the world are beginning to adopt the home cell group as an organizational tool.[26]

An example out of Singapore is Faith Community Baptist Church, founded by Pastor Lawrence Khong. Khong began the church in 1986 with 600 people. On May 1, 1988, with the help of Ralph Neighbour Jr., the church was restructured to become a full-fledged cell church. Today, the 7,000 members are pastored in 500 active cell groups. Khong's church so successfully models the cell-based ministry that 1,000 to 2,000 people attend its yearly cell seminar.

Pastors and church leaders all over the world have replicated Cho's cell system. Yet, far from simply imitating or copying other cell-based models, these churches have effectively adapted the model for their own situations and environments. New, creative patterns are emerging from these churches. Some actually are improvements on Cho's initial cell philosophy and demonstrate better integration between cell and celebration.[27]

With John Wesley leading the way and David Yonggi Cho bringing us up to date, cell churches now prevail throughout the world. In each of my case-study churches, the new cell leader immediately knew his mission—cell reproduction. Let's explore why some cell leaders are more successful than others in fulfilling that mission.

SUMMARY OF SURVEY FINDINGS

Factors that <u>don't</u> affect multiplication:
- The leader's gender, social class, age, marital (civil) status, or education.
- The leader's personality type.
  Both introverted and extroverted leaders multiply their cells.
- The leader's spiritual gifting.
  Those with the gift of teaching, pastoring, mercy, leadership, and evangelism equally multiply their cell group. This is surprising because many, including David Yonggi Cho, teach that only leaders with the gift of evangelism are able to multiply cell groups.

Factors that <u>do</u> affect multiplication:
- The cell leader's devotional time.
  Those who spend 90 minutes or more in devotions per day multiply their groups twice as much as those who spend less than 30 minutes.
- The cell leader's intercession for the cell members.
  Those who pray daily for cell members are most likely to multiply groups.

- The leader spending time with God to prepare for a cell meeting.
  Spending time with God preparing the heart for a cell meeting is more important than preparing the lesson.
- Setting goals.
  The leader who fails to set goals that the members remember has about a 50 percent chance of multiplying his or her cell. Setting goals increases that chance to 75 percent.
- Knowing your cell multiplication date.
  Cell leaders who set specific goals for giving birth consistently multiply their groups more often than goal-less leaders.
- Training.
  Cell leaders who feel better trained multiply their cells more rapidly. However, training is not as important as the leader's prayer life and goal orientation.
- How often the cell leader contacts new people.
  Leaders who contact five to seven new people per month have an 80% chance of multiplying the cell group. When the leader visits only 1 to 3 people per month, the chances drop to 60%. Leaders who visit eight or more new people each month multiply their groups twice as much as those who visit one or two.
- Exhortation in cell groups to invite friends.
  Cell leaders who weekly encourage members to invite visitors double their capacity to multiply their groups—as opposed to those leaders who do so only occasionally or not at all.
- Number of visitors to the cell.
  There is a direct relationship between the number of visitors in the group and the number of times a leader multiplies the group.
- Outside meetings.
  Those cells that have six or more social meetings per month multiply twice as much as those who have only one, or none.
- Raising up interns.
  Those leaders who gather a team double their capacity to multiply the cell.
- Level of pastoral care.
  Regular visitation by the leader to the cell members helps consolidate the group.

Prayer for Group Members:
- When comparing prayer, contacting, and social meetings, it was discovered that prayer for group members is the leader's most important work to unify and strengthen the group in preparation for multiplication. Building a team is a close second.

Preparation of the leader:
- When analyzing devotions, goals, training and preparation, devotions and goals are more important. Effective cell leadership is more of a Spirit-led adventure than a Bible-study technique.

Evangelistic thrust of the group:
- When analyzing visiting new people, exhortation, and visitors in the group, visitation and exhortation are equally important in the multiplication process. The flow of visitors is secondary.

SUMMARY OF KEY FACTORS ESSENTIAL FOR CELL MULTIPLICATION

- Factors essential to multiplying groups are leadership devotions, leadership outreach, group outreach, and building a team.
- Praying for team members and setting goals are primary in the first-time multiplication of a cell group.
- Leadership training and social meetings are necessary for continuous multiplication.

3

RELAX! YOU DON'T
NEED TO BE A SUPERSTAR

Many cell leaders say they don't have what it takes to lead a cell group. "I don't have the gift of evangelism." "I don't have the talent." "I'm too shy." Have you heard these before? Have you said them yourself? Such statements assume that a certain type of giftedness, personality, gender, social status, or education level is necessary to lead a cell. My findings refute such a notion.

LEADERSHIP GIFTEDNESS

The survey of 700 cell leaders in eight countries revealed absolutely no connection between the cell leader's spiritual giftedness and success in cell multiplication. Of five choices, the surveyed leaders chose their primary spiritual gift, and the results are:

Teaching	25.1%
Leadership	20.3%
Evangelism	19.0%
Pastoral care	10.6%
Mercy	10.6%
Other	14.4%

Table 2. Giftedness Among Cell Leaders

Surprisingly, 25 percent claimed teaching—not evangelism or leadership—as their primary gift. Also, no one particular gift correlated with a leader's capacity to multiply his or her group.

Perhaps this doesn't surprise you. But David Cho repeatedly teaches that only those cell leaders with the gift of evangelism can multiply cell groups.[1] His books make similar assertions.[2] For Cho, only those with the gift of evangelism can ultimately succeed, and he has concluded that only 10 percent of his congregation has this gift. If that is true, few will succeed in cell ministry.

What is the gift of evangelism? C. Peter Wagner gives this standard definition, "The gift of evangelist is the special ability that God gives to certain members of the Body of Christ to share the gospel with unbelievers in such a way that men and women become Jesus' disciples and responsible members of the Body of Christ."[3]

But cell churches worldwide are adopting a more revolutionary mode of reasoning that is borne out by the results of this survey. They increasingly are accepting that every lay person can successfully lead a cell group. For example, pastors at the International Charismatic Mission in Bogota, Colombia, exhort everyone who walks in the door to begin the cell leadership training process. This involves conversion, a spiritual retreat, a three-month training program, and another retreat before the person is released to lead. In October 1996, the church reported 6,000 cell groups. Just six months later, the cells had multiplied to 13,000.

Learning from the Bogota church, Bethany World Prayer Center recently adopted a similar mind-set. In a matter of months, Bethany's cell groups skyrocketed from 320 to 540. Bill Satterwhite, one of the zone pastors at Bethany, says that every person has the anointing for multiplication—no exceptions.

You, too, can successfully grow a cell group to the point of new birth. Spiritual gifts are important, but this statistical study and the experience of others demonstrate that no particular gift is necessary to lead a successful cell group. God anoints cell leaders with a variety of gifts. What you do as a leader matters more than your giftedness.

Successful small-group leaders take advantage of the variety of gifts within the cell. Remember that team ministry is highly valued in the small group. Perhaps one person on the team possesses the gift of teaching, another the gift of mercy, and still another leadership. All of these gifts help the group grow. The most successful cell groups involve the whole team—net fishing as a group rather than hook fishing as individuals.

Effective cell leaders excel in mobilizing the group to work together toward cell multiplication. Someone with the gift of helps will pick up new people and bring refreshments. The person with the gift of mercy will visit cell members or newcomers with the cell leader. Those with the gift of teaching work with the cell lesson. All are important, and everyone is involved and contributes to the group's success.

PERSONALITY

Carl Everett admits he is a shy person. You have to draw information from him, and he doesn't bubble over with enthusiasm. Communicating is not easy for him. Yet Carl is known as "Mr. Multiplication" at Bethany World Prayer Center. Carl started one cell group and watched it multiply. Then he mobilized the few remaining members to reach out until 15 "regulars" filled his group every Friday night. Again, the group gave birth to a daughter. Carl repeated this process six times before Bethany's top leadership, recognizing Carl's leadership, elevated him to shepherd cell leaders.

Potential cell leaders who tag themselves as "introverts" often say they lack the pizzazz or charisma to grow a healthy small group. But this survey shows that both extroverted and introverted leaders successfully multiply cell groups. More of these cell leaders are extroverted than introverted, but the important point is that the introverted cell leaders multiplied their cells on par with the extroverted.

When Jim Egli of TOUCH Outreach Ministries administered an expanded version of my questionnaire to 200 cell leaders at Bethany World Prayer Center, he included a question on the DISC Inventory personality types. (The DISC is a profile that measures primary and secondary personality strengths in terms of Dominant, Influencing, Steady, and Compliant.) He writes:

Interestingly, this initial research seems to show no strong correlation between DISC personality types and cell growth. 98 percent of Bethany's leaders had taken the DISC test and knew what their primary and secondary traits were, but no particular type performed better.[4]

All of this information confirms that you can be successful just as you are! God made you special. No one can do it quite like you. God uses the bubbly, the shy, the relaxed, the anxious, and all of the other personality types! Be yourself. It's not a matter of who you are as much as what you do as a cell leader.

OTHER NON-ESSENTIAL FACTORS

Does gender make a difference in cell-leader effectiveness? More than 80 percent of the cell leaders in David Cho's church are women. In fact, of the 62 who completed the questionnaire at Yoido Full Gospel Church, 58 are women and four are men. Does this mean that successful cell churches promote women leadership? Of the 700 cell leaders in my study, 51 percent are women and 49 percent men. The data reveals absolutely no difference between leadership effectiveness and gender. Both show equal success when asked how many times the group multiplied.

The average age of cell leaders in my study is 33, but no age bracket claims the leading edge with regard to cell multiplication. No significant pattern emerged as far as marital status, either.

What about occupation? White-collared cell leaders, blue-collared cell leaders, professionals, and teachers were equally capable of multiplying cell groups. What about education? Actually, the statistics seemed to indicate that less-educated cell leaders multiply more consistently and more often!

Cell leader, be encouraged. Whether you're male or female, educated or uneducated, married or single, shy or outgoing, a teacher or an evangelist, you can grow your cell group. The anointing for cell multiplication doesn't reside with just a few. These statistics reveal that gender, age, marital status, personality, and gifting have little to do with effectiveness as a cell leader. As we'll see in the following chapters, cell group growth depends on simple basics that anyone can put into practice.

4

PRAY!

One day a distraught Jorge Frias nervously opened the door to my office in Quito, Ecuador. "I've tried everything," he blurted out. "I've been addicted to alcohol, drugs, and even tried a couple of religions. Now my wife wants to leave me. What can you do for me?" Rarely had I witnessed such desperation in all my years of counseling. "I know that you've been sincerely seeking for answers," I said, "but only Jesus Christ can fill the void in your heart." As I led him in a prayer to receive Jesus Christ, the urgency in Jorge's voice finally ended in relief.

God took control of Jorge that day and he became a new creation. A radiance and joy flooded his life. Before he departed, I counseled Jorge to spend time with God daily—knowing that it might be a struggle for him.

At the new believer's class the next evening, Jorge said, "I woke up at 2 a.m. and prayed for 2-1/2 hours." That first night as a Christian, Jorge set prayer as a priority in his new life in Christ. He regularly spent two to four hours with Jesus in the morning. Within a year, Jorge was leading a cell group that he already had multiplied. He rapidly advanced from cell leader to supervisor to zone supervisor. Why? Because Jorge regularly gave God time to reveal to him how to effectively lead the groups.

THE DEVOTIONAL LIFE

The cell leader's devotional life consistently appears among the top three most important variables in this study. The correlation between cell multiplication and the leader spending time with God is clear. The cell leaders surveyed were asked: "How much time do you spend in daily devotions? (e.g., prayer, Bible reading, etc.)." They chose one of five options, ranging from 0 to 15 minutes daily to over 90 minutes. The following table summarizes the devotional patterns of those cell leaders who filled out a questionnaire:

0 to 15 minutes	11.7%
15 to 30 minutes	33.2%
30 to 60 minutes	33.8%
60 to 90 minutes	7.6%
90 minutes +	13.7%

Table 3. Devotional Patterns of Cell Leaders

In the same questionnaire, cell leaders were asked whether their group had multiplied and, if so, how many times. Those who spent 90 minutes or more in daily devotions multiplied their groups twice as much as those who spent less than half an hour.

The correlation is a logical one. During quiet times alone with the living God, the cell leader hears God's voice and receives His guidance. In those still moments, the leader understands how to deal with the constant talker, how to wait for a reply to a question, or how to minister to a hurting member of the group. Cell leaders moving under God's guidance have an untouchable sense of direction and leadership. Group members respond to a leader who hears from God and knows the way. God brings success. This statistical study is simply further proof of that.

Bobby Clinton writes,

A leader first learns about personal guidance for his own life. Having learned to discern God's direction for his own life in numerous crucial decisions, he can then shift to the leadership function of determining guidance for the group that he leads.[1]

He continues, "A leader who repeatedly demonstrates that God speaks to him gains spiritual authority."[2] It makes sense.

Daily devotional time is the single most important discipline in the Christian life. During that daily time, Jesus transforms us, feeds us, and gives us new revelation. On the other hand, not spending sufficient time with God can bring the agony of defeat. How often have we raced out of the house, hoping to accomplish a little bit more, only to return bruised, depressed, and hurt? When we start the day without time with our Lord, we lack power and joy to face the demands of life.

THE IMPORTANCE OF THE DEVOTIONAL LIFE

Jesus needed to spend time alone with His Father. How much more, then, do we? After all, He is our example. Luke 5:16 says, "… Jesus often withdrew to lonely places and prayed." Luke 5:15 explains that Christ's fame was spreading, and the success of his ministry compelled Him to spend more time with God. In the midst of an increasingly busy ministry, He separated from the multitude for quiet time. Mark 1:35 says, "Very early in the morning, while it was still dark, Jesus got up, left the house and went off to a solitary place, where he prayed." Before the busyness of His day began, Jesus spent time with the Father. Ralph Neighbour Jr. advises, "If you have to make a choice between praying and doing, choose to pray. You will accomplish more, and then achieve more by your doing, because you did!"[3]

The devotional patterns of some of the great men and women of God are well documented. Martin Luther confessed that he was so busy that he had to spend three hours in the morning with God. Historians tell us that John Welch often spent seven to eight hours each day in secret prayer. J.O. Frasier, a missionary to the Lisus tribes of western China, spent half his day in prayer and the other half in evangelism.[4] David Cho, who pastors the largest church in the history of Christianity (Yoido Full Gospel Church), attributes the growth of his church to the time spent in prayer.[5] John R. Mott, the driving force behind the North American Mission Movement in the last century, said,

After receiving Christ as Savior and Lord, and claiming by faith the fullness of the Spirit, we don't know of any other act that

produces so much spiritual blessing than keeping a regular devotional time for at least 1/2 hour, communing with God.[6]

God will reveal how much time He wants to spend with you each day. Effective cell leaders do not need to give up their job and family, and spend eight hours each day in prayer. At the other extreme, however, "fast food" devotions accomplish little. It takes time to shed the thoughts and preoccupations that accompany daily living. Mike Bickle writes:

> . . . When you first spend 60 minutes in a prayer time do not be surprised if you come out of it with only 5 minutes you consider quality time. Keep it up, and those 5 minutes will become 15, then 30, then more. The ideal, of course, is to end up with both quantity and quality, not one or the other.[7]

C. Peter Wagner writes in *Prayer Shield*, "My suggestion is: It is more advisable to start with quantity than quality in daily prayer time. First, program time. The quality will usually follow."[8] Wagner's suggestion smacks of reason. Cell leaders, if you want your group to grow, spend time with the One who can make it happen. Set a realistic goal you can keep rather than one you're sure to break.

A SPECIFIC TIME AND PLACE

Some Christians resist the notion of setting apart daily time to seek God. Some even say, "I pray all the time." Yes, the Bible tells us to pray without ceasing (1 Thessalonians 5:16), and Paul implores us to ". . . pray in the Spirit on all occasions with all kinds of prayers and requests" (Ephesians 6:18). But Jesus gives us the other side of the coin. Jesus says in Matthew 6:5-6, "And *when* you pray, do not be like the hypocrites, for they love to pray standing in the synagogues and on the street corners to be seen by men. I tell you the truth, they have received their reward in full, *but when you pray*, go into your room, close the door and pray to your Father, who is unseen." These verses map out a specific time set apart to seek the Father—a time to meditate on His Word, listen to the Spirit's voice, worship Him, and intercede for others.

When Jesus talks about a closet, he doesn't mean one full of shoes and clothing. The Greek word is *tameon*, and it refers to the place in the Old Testament temple where the treasures were stored. Some commentators note a relationship between the place of devotions and the riches received. Apparently, Jesus isn't specifying one place to seek the Father. More important than the word "closet" is the phrase "shut the door." Whether your "closet" is your room, the rooftop, a park, or a vacant field, you must "shut the door" from the noise and cares of daily life. Chuck Swindoll in *Intimacy with the Almighty* says, "Ours is a cluttered, complicated world. God did not create it that way. Depraved, restless humanity has made it that way!"[9] He goes on to say,

> *Tragically, precious little in this hurried and hassled age promotes such intimacy. We have become a body of people who look more like a herd of cattle in a stampede than a flock of God beside green pastures and still waters. Our forefathers knew, it seems, how to commune with the Almighty . . . but do we?*[10]

Jesus tells us to close the door to the noise and the hurry of busy 21st-century life.

How do you find a "closet" where you can shut the door? Be creative and experiment, and do the best you can. Some people prefer quite time in a forest or a park. Jesus preferred the desert or a mountain top. You choose the place and the time that is best for you. The only requirement is separation from the noise and confusion of life.

THE CONTENT

When you get together with a friend, do you list beforehand precisely what you are going to do and say? Of course not. You let the conversation ebb and flow, and just enjoy each other's company. That's how quiet time with God should be, too, but many Christians treat it as a ritual where they follow a set schedule or a devotional guide. Instead, think of it as a relationship. The goal is to know Him. The apostle Paul's yearning captures the heart of the devotional life: "I want to know Christ and the power of his resurrection and the fellowship of sharing in his suffering, becoming like him in his death" (Philippians 3:10).

If you're just not sure how to start your quiet time, begin by reading God's love letter to you—the Bible. Through the Word of God, the Holy Spirit nourishes our souls and grants guidance, so mine all of God's treasure. Offer praise to God. The writer of Hebrews says, "Through Jesus, therefore, let us continually offer to God a sacrifice of praise—the fruit of lips that confess his name" (13:15). Remember also to wait in silence before God. Ralph Neighbour Jr. refers to devotional time as the "listening room." He says that the cell leader "is first seeking to know the will of God concerning a situation. Prayer becomes a 'Listening Room' experience."[11]

But there is much more to prayer than spending time with the Lord in your "listening room." Cell leaders are intercessors who consistently pray for their cell members.

PRAY DAILY FOR CELL MEMBERS AND VISITORS

Of the many factors studied in this survey, the one with the greatest effect on whether a cell multiplies is how much time the cell leader spends praying for the cell members. This case study proves that daily prayer by the cell leader for the members is essential for a healthy, growing group. The survey asked cell leaders how much time they spend praying for the members of their group. The responses: Sixty-four percent pray daily for their cell, 16 percent every other day, 11 percent once a week, and 9 percent "sometimes." Comparing these answers with the data on cell multiplication confirms that cell leaders who pray daily for their members are far more likely to multiply cells than those who pray for them only once in a while.

Praying daily for cell members transforms your relationship with them. God uses prayer to change your heart toward the people for whom you are interceding. A oneness develops through the bonding power that prayer creates. Paul writes: "For though I am absent from you in body, I am present with you in spirit and delight to see how orderly you are and how firm your faith in Christ is" (Colossians 2:5). This verse seems to indicate that it's possible to be present "in spirit" with someone through prayer.[12] Prayer opens our hearts to others and enables us to touch people at a deeper level.

Regularly praying for someone can mend your broken relationship with that person. Through prayer, the healing balm of the Holy Spirit often breaks the strongholds of bitterness and unforgiveness. Prayer changes cells. Those cell leaders who pray daily for each member of the group are more effective in cell ministry.

When you speak with your cell members, tell them, "I'm praying daily for you." It develops an immediate bond with that person. In *Prayer Shield*, C. Peter Wagner details the necessity of intercessory prayer for Christian leaders, as well as how to recruit it.[13] Frankly, this book should be mandatory reading for everyone in cell leadership. Every level of church leadership needs to develop a prayer shield and also form part of someone else's prayer shield. Practically, this means that cell leaders pray daily for each person in their cell group. Section leaders pray daily for each cell leader in their section. Zone pastors pray daily for their section leaders; district pastors pray daily for their zone pastors. Finally, the senior pastor prays daily for the district pastors.

THE IMPEDIMENTS

Even knowing all of this, some cell leaders still struggle with the quality and quantity of their quiet time. Some people begin praying as soon as they awake—without getting out of bed. Deep prayer quickly turns into deep sleep. David Cho's advice about early morning devotions is: "Get out of bed!" Get up, wash your face, drink some coffee, and, if necessary, go for a jog or walk. Drowsiness is the number one enemy of effective devotions, so get the blood flowing.

Another impediment is our own thoughts. "What did that person think of my comments last night?" or "When should I wash my car?" Of course, we all have the same tendency. "Your thoughts, Lord, not mine!" is the battle of devotions.

How do you handle those ugly thoughts that worm their way into personal devotions? Should you try to pull them out as a dentist extracts a decayed tooth? Brother Lawrence did. As a Carmelite lay brother in the 17th century, he often battled a wandering mind. He wrote, "I worshiped Him the oftenest that I could, keeping my mind in His holy presence, and recalling it as often as I found it wandered from Him."[14]

But our own wrestlings often are so inadequate that only the Spirit of God can give full release. Ask Him to take over your thoughts in the listening room. The best remedy for roaming thoughts is to focus on Christ. As one looks at Jesus Christ, a new concentrated focus appears. A.W. Tozer once said, "The man who has struggled to purify himself and has had nothing but repeated failure will experience real relief when he stops tinkering with his soul and looks away to the perfect One."[15] Tozer's advice is relevant and helpful. As we give our thoughts to God and look to Him, He will refocus us and eventually fill us with His joy.

Another impediment is the busyness of our lives, frequently termed as "I don't have enough time." Leave the fast-food mentality with Burger King or McDonald's. In order to drink deeply from the Divine, you must spend time in deep meditation. As the Psalmist says, "Deep calls to deep" (Psalm 42:7). Andrew Murray counsels those entering into quiet time not to leave it without touching God, feeling the glow of the glory of God. Seeking Him at this level demands extended periods before God's throne. One or two short visits won't suffice.[16] It's no wonder that leaders capable of multiplying a cell group persevere with God first. Don't rob yourself of God's blessing by leaving His presence when He's about to fill you.

Jesus tells us that ". . . your Father, who sees what is done in secret, will reward you" (Matthew 6:6). Jesus reassures us here that the Father gives His rewards to those who live His way. Cell leaders, do you want the Father's reward? If you do it His way, God will enable you to lead the cell lesson with effectiveness, meet the spiritual needs of your people, and eventually multiply your group.

FASTING AND PRAYER

Carl Everett, now the assistant director of cell ministry at Bethany World Prayer Center, started out in ministry the way many other cell-church leaders do: leading a single cell group. His cell multiplied six times, and each daughter cell grew and prospered. Carl boils down the secret to his success into three words: "Prayer, prayer, prayer."

Cell preparation for Carl and his wife, Gaynel, includes fasting and prayer the day of the cell meeting. Before the meeting, they anoint the food, the sidewalks, the yard, every room in the house, even each seat to be used that night. Carl prays for the members and for God's anointing on his own life. They wait until after the meeting (during the refreshment time) before eating.

The Everetts' example is not unusual at Bethany, where cell leaders are encouraged to fast and pray before the cell meeting. Some fast the whole day; others until 3 p.m.; some may skip one meal. Carl says, "It is important to mobilize as many from the group as possible to fast and pray."

PRAYER WITHIN THE GROUP

Praying cells are powerful cells. The Holy Spirit is raising up a new prayer cell movement across the land,[17] and the cell church is strategically poised to lead it.[18]

Prayer fits naturally into the worship time of a cell meeting. Notice in Revelation 5:8-9 how prayer and worship blend together:

> *Each one had a harp and they were holding golden bowls full of incense, which are the prayers of the saints. And they sang a new song: 'You are worthy to take the scroll and to open its seals, because you were slain, and with your blood you purchased men for God from every tribe and language and people and nation.'*

As we see here, singing and prayer form part of the worship mix in the cell group. Both are essential to build the spiritual dynamic of the cell and to bring pleasure to Jesus Christ.

INTERCESSORY PRAYER IN THE CELL GROUP

Effective cell leaders pray aloud for cell members during the meeting. Let's use Marjorie, a successful cell leader, as an example. As she begins to pray for each member during the cell meeting, her pastor's heart is evident. Her prayers are so specific and personal, yet she doesn't reveal confidential matters. She warmly lifts each person in the meeting before the throne of God.

Marjorie has multiplied her group several times because she knows her flock, and they are willing to follow her. This type of prayer tells members that you care about them as individuals, helps establish your relationship with them, and ministers to their needs. This also is an excellent way for cell leaders to model intercessory prayer.

Part of the cell members' responsibility is to intercede for a world that doesn't know Jesus Christ. Each cell has its own Jerusalem (neighborhood), and it's probably best to begin there. Ralph Neighbour Jr. recommends writing the names of every relational contact on a large poster so the whole group can intercede in unison.[19] The Faith Community Baptist Church training manual exhorts potential cell leaders to, "Make mention of your unbeliever friends in the cell meetings. Encourage all the cell members to pray for them daily. God will answer these prayers."[20]

Along with praying for non-Christian friends, pray also for those who will start the new cell group. Avoid prayers of doubt here—"Lord, if it be your will to multiply this cell group . . ." The faithful cell member prays believing that multiplication is God's will (2 Peter 3:9-10; 1 Timothy 2:4-5). Floyd L. Schwanz addresses "How to Birth New Groups" in his book, *Growing Small Groups*. He counsels cell leaders to "get their group pregnant." How? Through prayer. He advises cell leaders to include a prayer in each week's meeting for those who will help start a new group. He says, "It gives the Holy Spirit an additional opportunity to work with the hearts of potential leaders."[21]

Yet, a cell's intercessory prayer also must invade the unreached people of the earth. God is calling His church worldwide to intercede on behalf of the unreached masses of the world, especially those living in the "10/40 Window." This is the geographical rectangle between 10 degrees and 40 degrees north latitude in which 90 percent of the unreached people groups live.

At Bethany World Prayer Center, cell groups conclude with intercessory prayer for the unreached peoples of the world. To that end, they've developed an excellent series of prayer profiles on unreached groups for other churches and cell groups to use.[22]

FLEXIBILITY IN PRAYER

Be creative! There is not one "right" way to mobilize cell members to pray, and flexibility helps avoid the boredom of a routine. Try these ideas:

- Break into groups of two or three. This allows more people to enter into prayer and is less intimidating for quieter members.
- Train your group to pray short, conversational prayers that provide greater interaction and agreement. This allows more people to pray and helps prevent one person from dominating.
- Ask individual cell members to intercede.
- Try using "concert prayer." C. Peter Wagner describes this as "all those present in the prayer meeting pray out loud at the same time."[23] Korean Christians have popularized this style of prayer. In Cho's church, the leader gives the signal to begin, and a roar of prayer floods the church until a bell signals that it's time to quit.

PRAYER IN CELL CHURCHES

Karen Hurston says, "Cells are simply the conduit through which the Holy Spirit flows; they are not an end in themselves." Sometimes we in the cell church movement forget that the cell is primarily a channel through which the Holy Spirit moves. Apart from His work, cells have little value.

Each church included in this case study earnestly seeks God's power through prayer. They promote prayer as the chief priority. Prayer is not just talked about; it's regularly practiced. For example, each of the churches hold regular all-night prayer meetings. The three largest cell churches in this study (35,000+ worshippers) hold weekly all-night prayer meetings.

The Living Water Church in Lima, Peru, gathers the church for fasting and prayer on seven of its country's 10 national holidays. Each such event draws about 1,000 people. The International Charismatic Mission also shines as a mighty example of prayer. From 5 to 9 every morning, praise choruses and fervent prayer rise from their building. Rare is the moment when one of the pastors or lay people is not preaching the Word of God, worshipping, or praying.

Sundays at Cho's Yoido Full Gospel Church are buzzing with life. From dawn until dusk, tens of thousands of people serve Jesus Christ in every nook and corner of that huge church.

What's the "secret strength" behind Yoido Full Gospel Church? Prayer. Some 3,000 people pray at Prayer Mountain each day (10,000 on the weekend). The leadership at YFGC believes that we are in a spiritual battle that can be won only in the heavenlies, and they act—and pray—accordingly. No wonder the evangelical church in Korea has grown from .05 percent to 30 percent of the population in a short period of time!

This spirit that pervades early morning prayer meetings is also central to the cell group at YFGC. Jeffrey Arnold sums up why David Yonggi Cho's church has grown so rapidly: "How did they grow so quickly? They encouraged each small group to pray for non-Christian friends, and they taught leaders how to lead people to Christ. With thousands of small groups in operation, each group bringing in a few new Christians every year or so created phenomenal growth."[24]

Until cell leadership is convinced that only God can convert a non-Christian and bring multiplication to the cell group, very little will happen. Ralph Neighbour Jr. says, "Trite moments of prayer in a cell group are incapable of breaking the spirit of lethargy in a cell."[25] It's like praying for food at a restaurant—mindless. Before prayer can make a difference in the cell, the cell leadership must "know that they know" that unless God breathes His life into our methodologies, they are just wood, hay, and stubble. When Jesus saw the pressing needs of the multitude, He didn't tell the disciples to initiate the latest evangelism-training program. Rather, he commanded them to "Ask the Lord of the harvest . . . to send out workers into his harvest field" (Matthew 9:38).

5

SET GOALS

If you aim for nothing, you'll definitely hit it! It's much easier to shoot the arrow first and *then* draw the bulls-eye around its landing spot. Far too many leaders take this approach, and the process is slow and haphazard. Clear-cut goals and cell success form an iron link. All eight churches in this case study set clear-cut goals at both the church and cell level.

The power of setting goals applies to successful leaders and growing churches in general. Kirk Hadaway, in *Church Growth Principles: Separating Fact from Fiction,* summarizes the results of his well-researched statistical study:

> *Growing churches are goal-directed. They set measurable goals for attendance, Sunday School classes, revivals, and for many other areas. . . . Setting goals helps churches to grow. . . . Goals provide direction and ensure that priorities (which flow out of purpose) are acted upon. . . . Challenging goals have the potential for producing motivation and enthusiasm. Big plans create a sense of excitement if they are consistent with the mission and vision of a congregation and are not seen as totally impossible.*[1]

True to form, the eight cell churches in this case study take a successful, goal-oriented approach to ministry and growth. One goal each cell strives toward is a target date for multiplication. The 700 cell leaders surveyed were asked, "Do you know when your group is going to multiply?" Possible answers were "yes," "no," or "not sure." Cell leaders who know their goal—when their groups will give birth—consistently multiply their groups more often than leaders who don't know. In fact, if a cell leader fails to set goals that the cell members clearly remember, he has about a 50-50 chance of multiplying his cell. But if the leader sets goals, the chance of multiplying increases to three out of four.

Ted Engstrom, a leader of leaders, observes, "The best leaders always had a planned course, specific goals, and written objectives. They had in mind the direction in which they wanted to go."[2] The same is true of the best cell leaders and churches.

CÉSAR CASTELLANOS

César Castellanos, pastor of the International Charismatic Mission in Bogota, Colombia, considers himself an apostle with an apostolic vision. His congregation knows that he spends large amounts of time in prayer and communion with the Holy Spirit. In those times, he receives his worldwide vision for the church. Like the apostles of old, Castellanos has successfully passed down his vision to his top leadership. Several of his key leaders attribute their own success to the vision and inspiration of their pastor.

Castellanos is a firm believer in short- and long-term goals. In October 1996, when the church had 5,600 cell groups, the church goal was to have 10,000 cell groups by December 31, 1996. At the time I wrote,

> . . . *The goals of the church were not adjusted to conform to reality. For example, the clearly stated goal of the church is to have 10,000 cell groups by the end of 1996. Two staff pastors told me they were sure that they were going to meet the goal even though it was only two months away. This would mean going from the present 5,600 cell groups to 10,000 cells in just two months. Practically speaking, this is humanly impossible.*

God majors in the "humanly impossible." Soon after my visit to the church, however, Pastor Castellanos marshaled his troops for one last thrust in 1996. The cell leaders were so enthused that they not only reached the goal of 10,000 groups but surpassed it by 600. As you can imagine, God humbled me and taught me about how He can use a leader with clear goals.

When one of God's leaders is filled with His vision, the Holy Spirit moves powerfully.

LUIS SALAS

One of the disciples of César Castellanos is Luis Salas. Luis is so serious about goals that he has a battle map, a list of multiplication goals. After reading his story, you'll understand why Castellanos often uses Luis as an example of amazing cell-group multiplication.

In June 1994 Luis began his first cell group, which grew to 30 persons. By September 1994, Luis gave birth to a daughter group that soon multiplied again. But beyond simply multiplying the group, Luis diligently trained members of the cell to start their own groups (which is the goal at International Charismatic Mission). By February 1995, Luis was overseeing 14 groups whose leadership he had discipled and pastored.

Pastor César Castellanos noticed Luis' progress and asked him to form part of the pastoral team. So in October 1995, Luis left his groups under the care of others while he began his new ministry directly under Castellanos. Three months later, Luis started from scratch once again. Within one month, his new cell group had grown from 10 to 60 people. This large group birthed several daughter cells, and by August the original cell had grown to 46 cells.

Luis and his disciples personally trained each of these 46 cell leaders. He knows that the only realistic way to meet his goal is to raise up new leaders, so he constantly looks for and trains emerging leaders. In October 1996, Luis was training 144 potential leaders. In November 1996, 86 cell groups were under Luis' care; one month later, 144 cells; in June 1997, 250 cells. In 18 months, Luis grew one cell of 10 people into 250 cells.

Is Luis sitting on his laurels? No way. He continues to set forth his future goals and details the steps needed to reach them.

Admittedly, Luis is a uniquely gifted cell leader. Not many possess his unique blend of vision, administration, and passion. But his example should inspire us, as William Carey said, "to expect great things from God and attempt great things for God."[3]

Luis lives in the future. Goals and dreams characterize his life. All effective leaders share this trait.

DAVID YONGGI CHO

David Yonggi Cho is extremely focused. He knows where his church is going and how it will get there. Cho says, "The number one requirement for having real growth—unlimited church growth—is to set goals."[4] He recommends four principles for setting goals:

1. Set specific goals.
2. Dream about those goals.
3. Proclaim those goals to the church.
4. Prepare for the fulfillment of the goals.

Cho believes that goal orientation is so essential to the success of cell ministry that the system would collapse without it. In his words, "Many churches are failing in their cell system because they do not give their people a clear goal and remind them constantly of their goal. If they have no goal, then the people will gather together and just have a grand fellowship."[5] He goes on to say, "Many people criticized me because I was giving goals to my people then encouraging them to accomplish the goals. But if you don't give them a goal, they will have no purpose to being in the cell."[6]

Notice that the goal is cell-group evangelism that results in multiplication. With 25,000 cell leaders setting clear multiplication goals, is it any wonder that the Yoido Full Gospel Church is the largest church in the history of Christianity?

EFFECTIVE CELL CHURCHES KNOW WHERE THEY'RE GOING

It's amazing how goal orientation pervades every level of the cell church. Love Alive in Honduras, which exploded beyond 1,000 cells in 1997, is a good example. Dixie Rosales, the director of cell ministry, explains that he and René Penalba (the head pastor) determine the number of cell groups each year. He considers this job simple because every leadership level determines its own goals that are then combined into an overall goal:

1. The cell leaders communicate their goals for multiplication to the area supervisors.
2. The area supervisors tell their zone pastors how many cell groups under their care will be ready to give birth.
3. The zone pastors tell the district pastors how many possible new births to expect in their zones.
4. The district pastors communicate their goals and visions to the director of the cell groups.
5. The director of cell groups, in coordination with the district pastors, establishes a multiplication goal for the year. The pastoral team then approves this goal.

At Elim Church in El Salvador, multiplication goals are updated weekly and posted to show which leaders are closest to reaching their goals (the goal for every leader is 100 percent multiplication). Obviously, no one wants to be on the bottom of the list. The "healthy competition" that exists among the pastors spurs a high degree of motivation to grow.

GOALS AND VISION

Multiplication does not happen naturally. In fact, just the opposite often occurs. The actual tendency is for cell groups to look inward. Close relationships have developed; fun times have been shared. Why should the cell even think about forming a new one?[7] *Home Cell Groups and House Churches* reports,

> *The principle of cell division and growth seems critical here to help avert the problem of exclusiveness. . . . The purpose of such action is designed to prevent the kind of exclusiveness and inwardness that can eventually undermine one of the most significant goals of cell groups—outreach and growth.*[8]

It is precisely at this point of "turning inward" that without a vision for growth the people perish (Proverbs 28:19). This vision can only come from leadership—the section leaders, cell leaders and interns. Leaders casting the vision fan the flame and keep the goal alive. Vision, like faith, sees things that are not as though they were. In *The Power of Vision*, George Barna writes:

Vision is a picture held in your mind's eye of the way things could or should be in the days ahead. Vision connotes a visual reality, a portrait of conditions that do not exist currently. This picture is internalized and personal.[9]

Effective leaders meditate on their vision and clarify it so they can share it with others. "Leaders are only as powerful as the ideas they can communicate," according to *Leaders: The Strategies for Taking Charge.*[10] Though not an easy task, leaders step out in faith to constantly communicate to their cells that they *will* multiply. They believe in the vision of reaching out to others and bringing them to know Jesus, and God guides them toward fulfilling it. While some cell members embrace cell multiplication for the purpose of fulfilling Christ's Great Commission, others talk about cell division in a negative light. The leader makes the difference in how the group views growth and multiplication.

It's somewhat like the story about two shoe salesmen who went to Africa. Both of them noticed that very few people wore shoes. One wired back to his home office: "Our company has no future here. There is no market for our product. No one wears shoes." The other salesman fired off a wire as follows: "We have a gold mine of a market here. Everyone needs shoes!"[11]

In commenting on the miracle of David Cho's church growth—how it grew from 20 small groups to over 20,000 small groups—C. Kirk Hadaway says, ". . . the numbers continued to grow because a growth strategy was built into each cell group."[12] This "built-in strategy" or "genetic code" is planted through the cell leader's vision and dreams. Karen Hurston talks about one cell leader named Pablo, who shares with the group his vision for multiplication before every meeting. The people in Pablo's group have a very positive idea about cell-group multiplication. They see the multiplication of their group as a sign of success.[13]

Vision explains why Freddie Rodriguez succeeds. In 1987, Freddie became a convert and disciple of César Fajardo, the youth leader at the International Charismatic Mission in Bogota. ICM operates under the "Groups of Twelve Model," which emulates the way Jesus formed His cell group of 12. By 1990, Freddie had found his 12 disciples who were all leading cell groups. Those 12 sought and found 12 more, and the process continued. As of March 1997, Freddie was directly responsible for more than 900 cell groups. He continues to meet with his original 12 every week, and he also meets with about 500 of his leaders on a weekly basis.

Cell leader, pray and dream about your cell group. Ask God to show you His desire for the group. It is unwise for cell leaders to do the work of the ministry at the expense of their time with the Lord. And working without a God-given goal often proves futile. Perhaps this is why leaders who spend more time before God are more effective in cell multiplication. They've received God's vision for the cell group. Barna says, ". . . the vision-capturing process may be an ordeal. Hours and hours will be spent in prayer, in study. . . . Some leaders find this period very lonely."[14] But, undoubtedly, very fruitful in the end.

GOALS AND PRAGMATISM

Donald McGavran, the founder of the church-growth movement, teaches that church growth is simply catching the fish (evangelism) and not letting them go (discipleship in the church). McGavran's passion for the lost propelled him to promote an uncompromising pragmatism. He writes:

Nothing hurts missions overseas so much as continuing methods, institutions, and policies which ought to bring men to Christ—but don't; which ought to multiply churches—but don't; which ought to improve society—but don't. If it does not work to the glory of God and the extension of Christ's church, throw it away and get something which does. As to methods, we are fiercely pragmatic—doctrine is something entirely different.[15]

All of the above leads us to this point: There is no ultimate "right way" to multiply your cell group. The "right way" for you is the one that edifies the saints and attracts non-Christians to your group. Goals and dreams propel a cell leader to make it happen, however the job gets done—within Biblical guidelines, of course. Successful cell leaders translate intention into reality and then sustain it.[16] If a cell leader has multiplied the group, he or she has done it the "right way." This attitude characterized the life and ministry of John Wesley. Richard Wilke notes:

> *John Wesley changed his structures and methods, almost against his will, in order to save souls. He didn't want to use women, but he did in exceptional circumstances. The 'exceptional' became normal. He didn't want to use lay pastors, but he did. They were able to reach the unbelievers. He didn't want to preach in the open air, but he did so that more might hear the Word of God.*[17]

Tom Peters takes pragmatism one step farther. "The best leaders . . . are the best 'note-takers,' the best 'askers,' the best learners. They are shameless thieves."[18] Peters recommends the "Swiped from the Best with Pride"[19] methodology that will ultimately lead to the multiplication of the cell group.

Successful cell leaders know where they're going and how to get there because they hear from the Master. Effective cell leadership is not based on gimmicks and techniques. It's grounded in spending time with God until He provides clear direction and guidance. Ultimately, He grants success.

Your church can grow rapidly, too. The key is cell leaders who pray and have been instilled with a goal-oriented mentality. Each of Cho's leaders is to know when the group will give birth (it is preferable to have the exact date).[20] Ralph Neighbour gives similar instruction, "Cell leaders will set a goal for doubling the cell in a given period of time. These goals can be reached as the Holy Spirit anoints people like yourself. . . . Someone has said, 'I'd rather shoot at a goal and miss it than shoot at nothing, and hit it!'"[21]

6

RAISE UP
NEW LEADERS

The phrase "urgent evangelism" expresses two things: (1) Scripture's teaching on the fate of those who don't know Jesus and (2) the necessity of believers to share the gospel of Christ. An "urgent" matter takes precedence over other concerns, and Jesus clarified His priority on earth when he said, "For the Son of Man came to seek and to save what was lost" (Luke 19:10).

Christ's priority remains an urgent one. He said, "Do you not say, 'Four months more and then the harvest'? I tell you, open your eyes and look at the fields! They are ripe for harvest" (John 4:35). Commenting on this passage, Matthew Henry says, "Harvest time . . . will not last always; and harvest work is work that must be done then or not at all . . . it was necessary work, and the occasion for it very urgent and pressing."[1]

Scripture teaches that the world is eternally lost (John 3:36; 2 Thessalonians 1:7-9, 16; Jude 23). Paul was compelled to preach the gospel (1 Corinthians 9:16) and persuade people with the good news of Jesus Christ because every person will stand before the judgment seat of Christ (2 Corinthians 5:11). He writes in Romans 10:14, "How, then, can they call on the one they have not believed in? And how can they believe in the one of whom they have not heard? And how can they hear without someone preaching to them?" That's a message of urgency.

We are at war over the eternal matter of people's souls. The prince of darkness recognizes that he and his demon forces have a very short time (Revelation 12), and these evil forces strive to blind and deceive as many people as possible. God calls His church to defeat the enemy by winning people to Jesus. Some Christians wage war by themselves, but the cell church methodology is group-oriented. Each cell is a guerrilla team to reach the lost. Cell groups realize from the start that they are called to fulfill a goal greater than themselves—reaching the lost for Jesus Christ. This drives the cell as a unit and unites it under one purpose.

"Urgent evangelism" in the cell church results in conversions, and thus in rapid cell multiplication. Numerical growth is intentionally planned and aggressively pursued. The sole motivation for growth in the eight case-study churches is the eternal state of those who don't know Jesus. These churches don't debate the "numbers game." They seek the lost for eternal reasons.

SEE EVERYONE AS A MINISTER

Paul writes in Ephesians 4:11-12 that God gifted church leadership for the purpose of training the laity to do the work of the ministry. The goal of leadership, therefore, is "to prepare God's people for works of service, so that the body of Christ may be built up." John echoes this truth in Revelation 1:6 when he says that Christ made us to be a kingdom of priests.

As children of the Reformation, we agree with the concept that every Christian is a minister. But that doesn't necessarily mean that we live it. Many in the United States ask, "Why hasn't the cell church mushroomed in the U.S. like it has in Korea?" Larry Kreider, founder of DOVE Christian Fellowship, asked David Cho that very question. Cho didn't hesitate: "The problem here in America is that pastors are not willing to release their lay people for ministry."[2] Cho is referring to the hesitancy of pastoral leadership in the U.S. to delegate pastoral authority to their cell leaders and interns.

In one sense, this hesitancy is understandable. No pastor wants to be accused of shallowness, or of emphasizing quantity over quality. Also, the majority of pastors in the U.S. have passed through a system of extensive, formal training. It is natural, therefore, and even logical for them to expect potential lay leadership to pass through similar formal training. And, yes, there are merits to this type of pre-service training. It certainly weeds out the non-committed and assures that potential leaders become thoroughly acquainted with sound Christian doctrine.

This approach, however, has two fatal errors. First, it fails to acknowledge that the best learning is caught, not taught. Leadership learning is a process, so potential leaders cannot be "perfected" before they're sent into ministry. Leaders gain vital experience as they make mistakes, reflect on them, and chart mid-course corrections. The cell group is, in fact, the perfect laboratory. Carl George says, "The best possible context anyone has ever discovered for developing leadership occurs because of a small group."[3]

The second flaw concerns the work of the Holy Spirit. A philosophy that relies on formal training for cell leadership often minimizes the power of, and the reliance on, the Holy Spirit. Take the example of the apostle Paul. During the first century, Paul established churches throughout the Mediterranean and left them in the hands of relatively new Christians.[4] He trusted the Holy Spirit to work through these young leaders. Speaking of Paul's method, Roland Allen writes:

> *The moment converts were made in any place ministers were appointed from among themselves, presbyter Bishops, or Bishops, who in turn could organize and bring into the unity of the visible Church and new group of Christians in their neighborhood.*[5]

Unlike Paul, we often hang educational nooses around the necks of potential leaders, thinking that only those trained to our specifications can minister. Paul trusted the Holy Spirit to work in the lives of new believers and developing leaders. As David Sheppard points out, "We've settled for the priesthood of all educated believers."[6] The rest of the saints just sit and listen Sunday after Sunday. Aubrey Malphurs pinpoints the problem:

> *The great tragedy is that far too many Christians are either not involved or not properly involved in any service for Christ or His church. . . . According to a survey by George Gallup . . . only 10 percent of the people in the church are doing 90 percent of the ministry of the church. Thus, 90 percent of the people are*

typically unemployed 'sitters and soakers.' Of the 90 percent, approximately 50 percent say they'll not become involved for whatever reason. The remaining 40 percent say they'd like to become involved, but they've not been asked or trained.[7]

The "unemployment" of the laity is a serious issue facing the church today. The typical Sunday morning "teaching-and-preaching" ministry does not involve many lay people. Only very "gifted" and "highly educated" people are allowed to participate. Hadaway writes, "The clergy-dominated Christianity of the Western world has widened the gap between clergy and laity in the body of Christ. This division of labor, authority, and prestige is common when a professional clergy exists."[8]

God's agenda of "urgent evangelism" demands participation by all His people. The time for a chosen few to do the work of ministry has passed. This is, instead, the time to trust the Holy Spirit to work among the entire Body of Christ. Instead of relying on our own expertise, education and experience, we must trust God to work through others as we equip and release them to lead.

DECENTRALIZE THE MINISTRY

In cell churches, ministry is taken out of the hands of a "chosen few" and placed in the lap of many. Unlike in a large celebration service, everyone is encouraged to participate in cell groups and use their spiritual gifts. Peter reminds us that ". . . one should use whatever gift he has received to serve others, faithfully administrating God's grace in its various forms" (1 Peter 4:10). No one sits passively. Everyone must be involved.

This type of decentralization spurs the rapid multiplication at International Charismatic Mission, where layers of machinery that hinder lay involvement have been removed. Pastor César Castellanos says ICM's goal is to make a cell leader out of every person who enters the church. He invites potential cell leaders to the altar during celebration services. If cells are going to multiply rapidly, new leaders must constantly be sought and released.

Cell groups are "leader breeders."[9] Hadaway writes, ". . . small home-centered groups provide the intimate atmosphere . . .

conducive to maximum leadership development."[10] For this reason, cell churches are in a unique position to maximize lay involvement. Elevating new leadership must have high priority. Pastor Castellanos tells his leaders not to "recruit" cell members but to "train" leaders. The success of the cell church depends on transforming lay people into lay leaders. That is the force behind the home cell group explosion. The goal of every cell leader, therefore, is to raise up new leadership. Many cell leaders fail at precisely this point, because the primary focus of leadership development becomes blurred with the burdens of attracting new people, perfecting the lesson content, or honing the worship.

The Cell Leader as Pastor

Cell leaders also are pastors. Some people have trouble calling cell leaders "pastors," but they fulfill every biblical principle of a pastor. In John Wesley's system of small groups, the class leaders were pastors. Pastoring involves five main principles.

1. Care for the Sheep (Acts 20:28-29).
The cell leader visits, counsels, and prays for the sick flock. The cell leader is responsible for caring for the cell as a shepherd cares for his flock. Karen Hurston's long involvement with Yoido Full Gospel Church in Seoul, Korea, convinced her that cell leader visitation is paramount.

2. Know the Sheep (John 10: 14,15).
Effective cell leaders get to know each person who enters the group. Ralph Neighbour Jr. recommends that the cell leader talk one-on-one with new members, using a booklet called *The Journey Guide* to facilitate this initial interview.[11] He exhorts:

> *Nothing can substitute for personal time with each member of your flock! It will be in such private times that you will discern their value systems and deepest needs. While you will usually have your Intern at your side when you visit, there will be times when more private sessions may help you gain special insights into each person.*[12]

3. Seek the Sheep (Luke 15:4).

Jesus talks about leaving the flock of 99 sheep to seek the one that has gone astray. Knowing that a satanic-dominated world is always working against godliness in the lives of the cell members, a true shepherd goes after the sheep who stop attending.

4. Feed the Sheep (Psalm 23: 1-3).

The cell group is not a Bible study, but the Word of God always has a central place. Many meetings are based on practical application of a scripture passage, and leaders preparing for the cell often meditate on a passage longer than they would if they were leading a Bible study or Sunday School. They must know it well enough to lovingly draw the group into clear understanding of how the Bible applies to their daily lives. In this way, the sheep are fed and leave the cell group satisfied.

5. Watch Out for the Sheep (John 10:10, Ephesians 6:12).

Satan walks about like a roaring lion hoping to devour God's flock (1 Peter 5:8-9). In many churches, Satan has free reign to attack because the people are not cared for properly. In the cell church, every 10 or so members are under the care and guidance of the cell pastor and intern, who are responsible for protecting their sheep. Paul's advice to the pastors in Ephesus is helpful to every cell leader:

> *Keep watch over yourselves and all the flock of which the Holy Spirit has made you overseers. Be shepherds of the church of God, which he bought with his own blood. I know that after I leave, savage wolves will come in among you and will not spare the flock. Even from your own number men will arise and distort the truth in order to draw away disciples after them. So be on your guard! (Acts 20:28-31)*

We're reminded here that Satan doesn't attack only from without. He also raises up self-proclaimed leaders in Christian small-group gatherings to create division and to attract a following. Problem people are common in small groups, and the cell shepherd must be diligent about ensuring that their behavior does not negatively affect his flock.

PASTOR THOSE IN THE GROUP

The survey also asked the cell leaders: "As the leader of the cell group, how many times per month do you contact the members of your group?" More than 700 responses provided these results: 25 percent, one to two times per month; 33 percent, three to four; 19 percent, five to seven; and 23 percent, eight or more. That's right: 23 percent of the cell leaders in this study visit their cell members eight or more times per month. As might be expected, leaders who visit cell members more often multiply the cell group more times. A personal visit demonstrates the pastoral care of the cell leader and often converts cell members into cell workers.

BE WILLING TO MULTIPLY LEADERSHIP

If you're uncomfortable with the concept of "lay pastors," remember that cell leaders and interns are not Bible teachers. Their job description is pastoral.[13] Instead of teaching a Bible lesson, cell leaders guide the communication process, pray for the group, visit cell members, and reach lost people for Christ. Carl George succinctly says, "In the church of the future a leader won't be known for his or her ability to handle a quarterly or written study guide so much as for a skill in relating to people in such a way that they allow access into their lives."[14]

Growing cell churches successfully equip their leadership, using both pre-service and ongoing training. Pastoral leadership in the cell church must rely on the Holy Spirit to work through those who desire to serve Jesus, show enthusiasm and have a clear testimony.[15] As God raises up potential leaders, they need to be recognized as such by the cell leaders. Again, David Cho is an example of someone who obviously does that. Even in a church of 700,000+ members, Yoido Full Gospel Church maintains an average of one lay leader for every 10 to 16 church members.[16] For example, in 1988 alone, 10,000 new lay leaders were appointed for ministry.[17]

When asked where all the leaders for thousands of new cell groups come from, Cho immediately reports, "We get them from our new Christians."[18] Another pastor whose leaders come from this camp is Pete Scazzero, who oversees a growing C&MA cell church in New York. He says:

Our future is limited by our leadership. . . . Several of the cell-group leaders and apprentices are new Christians. Young Christians who lead cell groups grow like crazy . . . especially as they learn to base their identity in Christ instead of in their ministries or on their egos.[19]

The Latin American churches used in this case study confirm Scazzero's findings. The research indicates that newer Christians tend to multiply their groups faster than those who have been believers for a longer period. Is this because new Christians still have non-Christian contacts? Too many "mature Christians" lose touch with their non-Christian contacts. These findings show that as cell leaders watch their members carefully to identify and develop emerging leaders, they cannot afford to overlook the new converts. Watch members grow, and listen for guidance from the Holy Spirit. If you as the cell leader make leadership development your chief goal, you are on the way to successful cell group multiplication.

CONTINUALLY PRAY FOR MORE LEADERS

Leadership development and deployment is first and foremost a divine task. Only God can raise up an anointed, effective leader. Jesus instructed his disciples this way, "The harvest is plentiful but the workers are few. Ask the Lord of the harvest, therefore, to send out workers into his harvest field" (Matthew 9:37-38). We must remember that God is working behind the scenes to develop new leaders.

Prayer touches the heart of God and changes our own hearts. It produces within us a constant watchfulness for potential leadership. Prayer gives us God's perspective and erases our own preconceived standards. That person you see today as stumbling and fumbling might be the next district pastor—if given the opportunity. God's counsel to Samuel is a constant reminder to us: "Do not consider his appearance or his height, for I have rejected him. The Lord does not look at the things man looks at. Man looks at the outward appearance, but the Lord looks at the heart" (1 Samuel 16:7). Purity of heart, faithfulness, and willingness to work hard are far more important in cell ministry than natural talent, social status, or charisma.

INVOLVE POTENTIAL LEADERS

The next step after praying for potential leaders is to involve them in the cell meeting. Because your cell meeting is a training ground for new leadership, ask Mary to lead the ice-breaker next week. Or invite Jim to lead worship. Eventually, someone else will facilitate the lesson. People learn in the process of doing, so allow your members to get involved.

Avoid placing titles on potential leaders in the beginning. Jesus called his disciples to follow Him before he officially gave them titles (Mark 1). Be sure that a certain person is the right one to lead the next cell group before putting a title on him or her. This enables you to select the right person, but it will also produce more leaders. People will be more willing to wear the title if they've tasted and enjoyed the leadership experience.

TEST FAITHFULNESS

Potential cell leaders need to prove themselves in the small things. Jesus says in Luke 16:10, "Whoever can be trusted with very little can also be trusted with much, and whoever is dishonest with very little will also be dishonest with much." Faithfulness is essential to cell leadership. People forgive quirks and weaknesses, but those who are unfaithful or irresponsible automatically are removed from leadership. This means that a potential leader must be proven more than once. Give people several chances to perform a particular task. Don't label anyone as unfaithful just because they fail to bring the refreshments one night. Give them several opportunities.

People learn best by taking incremental steps. That is, the successful completion of a smaller task helps them gain confidence for a larger one. Begin by asking the person to read scripture, pray, or organize refreshments. Note whether the task is completed successfully. If it isn't, talk directly with that person because transparency and honesty are the best policy. If it is carried out properly, give greater responsibility next time.

CONSULT WITH OTHERS

You as the cell leader are in the best position to involve and recruit new leadership. But don't do it alone. The writer of Proverbs counsels, "For lack of guidance a nation falls, but many advisers make victory sure" (11:14). To ensure victory in choosing your interns, consult with the leaders over you (e.g., discipler, supervisor, zone pastor). They will confirm your decisions most of the time, but you want to make sure. They might know something you don't. One of the beauties of the cell church is the multiplicity of cell leadership that assures quality control.

RECRUIT THE NEW LEADER

When you are sure that you have found the right one(s), make contact. Follow the example of Jesus, who called his disciples personally and directly. Go over to the person's house, school, or work—make it a special meeting. Important meetings are normally planned and well thought out. The potential new leader needs to know that the decision was deliberate and premeditated. And don't withhold praise for fear of "puffing them up." Every small encouragement works wonders as new leaders face fears and uncertainties over talent, spiritual giftedness, and weaknesses. Affirm any and all positive qualities. All of us yearn to know that we do something well. A good rule of thumb is to give more praise than criticism. Before you offer advice, ask interns whether they see any need for improvement. Let them mention obvious weaknesses before you do. This will allow you to see how they perceive things as it strengthens your role as an encourager.

INCREASINGLY TURN MINISTRY OVER TO THE NEW LEADER

The example of Jesus is instructive for cell ministry. Jesus showed His disciples how to do the ministry; he ministered along side them. He modeled effective ministry while the disciples watched and participated. Jesus then went one step further—he sent the disciples out to do some work by themselves (Matthew 10:5-20). Finally, after thorough training, Jesus left them completely (Acts 1:11).

Six months usually is sufficient time for you to develop a new leader to shepherd a cell. You may raise up cell leadership more rapidly or it might take longer, but make it your goal to prepare the new leader in six months. If you've done it right, the new cell leader should be able to lead a daughter cell, plant a new cell, or continue leading your group (while you start a new one).

TRAIN YOUR LEADERSHIP FULLY

Cell church training is more like preparing a lightning task force than a standing army. New leaders soon may be on the front line, and this reality mandates relevant training that is practical, workable, and usable in the same week.

All of the cell churches in this study have clearly defined requirements for potential cell leaders. Although these requirements vary from church to church, the core requirements include:

1. Salvation
2. Water baptism
3. Cell attendance
4. Completion of a cell training course.[20]

Although the length and demands of the cell training course varies, two characteristics are similar: (1) it is taught by pastoral staff and (2) it always covers cell organization, cell vision, and New Testament leadership requirements. Cell churches that raise up leadership quickly, yet effectively, maintain both the quantitative and qualitative edge. Both are essential.[21]

A few key ingredients are always present in churches with cell leader training models:

1. Some kind of pre-training for cell leaders.
2. A Jethro system in which every leader is pastored.[22]
3. On-going training.
4. An intentional way for emerging leaders to be spotted, encouraged, and integrated into the leadership structure.

The pressing question about training models is, "Which model best serves the multiplication process?" No one does it better than the International Charismatic Mission.

LEADERSHIP TRAINING AT ICM

ICM estimates that it keeps the majority of new converts because of its follow-up and training program. César Fajardo, the pastor at ICM responsible for raising up more than 3,600 youth cell groups, says that the key to his success is quality leadership, which results in amazing church growth. This is what ICM's training looks like.

FIRST ENCOUNTER RETREAT

These are regular spiritual retreats designed to ensure that the people who accept Christ during an altar call have experienced the Christian life. During the Encounter, each person receives concentrated teaching about liberation from sin, the sanctified life, and the baptism of the Holy Spirit. This is the first step toward becoming a leader at ICM.

FIRST SEMESTER OF LEADERSHIP SCHOOL

Next, the potential leader attends C.A.F.E. 2000, "Cells of Family Training and Evangelism." The training material gives the potential leader the basic foundational principles for leading a small group.[23] These leadership-training meetings take place throughout the week. In October 1996, about 15 leadership training schools were in session every day with an average of 30 students per class and a total of some 3,000 students.

SECOND ENCOUNTER RETREAT

After the young people ministry proved the effectiveness of a second Encounter Retreat, other ICM departments also began requiring this next step.[24] This second retreat is designed to reinforce the commitments made at the first retreat and to instill more principles in the potential leader before he or she launches the cell group.

SECOND AND THIRD SEMESTER
OF LEADERSHIP SCHOOL

The core cell leadership training lasts three months, but the deeper levels of training extend to nine months. During this second and third semester, there is deeper level teaching about false cults and false philosophies, and about ICM's core values. By the time students enter the second semester, they are leading a cell group. This forces the student to learn both theoretically and practically, which might explain the school's high rate of attrition. It is normal for the first three-month session to begin with 40 students, drop to 35 in the second trimester, and end up with only 22 by the last trimester.

FLET

If a leader desires deeper levels of training beyond these nine-month courses, an excellent course called FLET (*Facultad, Latino, Entrenimiento, Teologica:* the faculty of Latin America Theological training) is offered. Although FLET is not emphasized at ICM as a required course for continued leadership training, it does give the opportunity for leaders to continue in their theological training.

BUILD A CELL LEADERSHIP TEAM

We've looked at identifying and growing new leaders. Many cell churches take this process one more step, forming them into a leadership team—the nucleus of the cell. The nucleus contains the genetic code for duplication, so multiplying the leadership team ensures strong, ongoing daughter cells. Successful leaders reach into the cell and build the leadership team.[25]

Cell leaders in the eight case study churches were asked: "How many assistant leaders do you have in your group?" Their four choices ranged from zero to three or more. From the total number of respondents: 21 percent did not have an assistant leader, 35 percent had one, 17 percent had two, and 29 percent had three or more. Comparing the number of assistants to how well the cells multiply shows that cell leaders with three or more assistant leaders double their capacity to multiply the cell group. When compared to the other significant variables in this study, this factor ranked highest in helping cell leaders multiply their group several times.

The question didn't draw out all the needed information about team ministry. For example, some cell groups recognize only one assistant leader while calling the other team members by different names (e.g., treasurer, children's leader, disciple, and "members at large"). More information about team ministry was gathered in the case-study churches, though, and it's clear that team-building is a crucial focus of the cell leader. Let's take a more in-depth look at two Latin American cell churches that are particularly adept at applying the team model.

LOVE ALIVE

The Love Alive Church in Tegucigalpa, Honduras proves that team ministry is "alive and well" in the cell church today. A new cell can be birthed at Love Alive only when a new team is in place. Ninety percent of the 1,000 cell groups there have leadership teams instead of solo leaders. The new team members, or "missionaries" as they commonly are called, are carefully selected, trained, and sent out.

Most new teams consist of three principal members—the leader, the intern, the treasurer—and two members at large. Before the cell multiplies, the new leader (the intern leader in the mother cell) is actively involved in the mother group, preparing to lead the new cell. The new treasurer helps count the money collected in the cell and delivers it to the church each week.[26] Any member of the leadership team, including the two members at-large, is allowed to fulfill any role in the cell.

Each cell team (whether in the mother or daughter cell) meets apart from the regular cell group at least once a month to strategize. After every celebration service, the leadership teams meet. The supervisors and cell teams gather in designated locations in the church to pray, plan, evaluate their progress, and encourage each other. Each leader, from members at-large to district pastors, are held accountable for their attendance.

ELIM

Elim Church in El Salvador also believes in team ministry. The team consists of the leader, assistant, host, treasurer, secretary, instructor of children, and members at large. The cell leader's primary goal is to form this core team. Elim Church is convinced that the success of the cell group depends on the nucleus.

Elim believes so strongly in team ministries that the core team (and some potential leaders) meets weekly to plan, pray, dream, and act. After a time of edification, team members plan for the normal Saturday night cell meeting. They decide who will visit straying members, reach new people, and pray for those in need. Multiplication of the cell group is envisioned, and the new team begins to take shape.

Having two separate cell meetings (one for planning and one for outreach) is the major distinction between the cell system at Elim and those at other cell churches. Elim's cells are top quality, and gathering the core team on a regular basis for planning, prayer, and vision-casting appears to be a key factor.

Don't Fear Failure

Not all cell groups successfully raise up new leaders and multiply. It's not the end of the world if a cell dissolves, because important principles are learned in the process. The cell leader and members are encouraged to attend a group that is better prepared for the task.

Successful leaders learn from their failures, becoming stronger as a result: ". . . for the successful leader, failure is a beginning, the springboard of hope."[27] Soichiro Honda, the founder of Honda Motor, writes:

> *Many people dream of success. To me success can only be achieved through repeated failure and introspection. In fact, success represents the 1 percent of your work which results only from the 99 percent that is called failure.*[28]

In *Thriving on Chaos*, Tom Peters states that companies should promote failure. He counsels executives to hold "Hall of Shame" parties, to give rewards to those who have fouled up recently and to share freely about their own failures.[29] Peters promotes the motto of "fast failure": "Fail and get on with it!" He reasons that the freedom to make mistakes results in innovation and progress.

This principle has huge implications for the cell church. The ever-expanding needs of the cell church demand the involvement of lay leadership. After all, every leader starts somewhere. Some leaders will fail and choose to withdraw, and some groups will be dissolved. This is to be expected. The majority of leaders, however, will learn from their mistakes, correct them, and press on. With the proper control and administration over the cell groups, the vast majority succeed.

7

ATTRACT VISITORS

S uccessful cell leaders serve by reaching out, but they can effectively do this only through their life-giving relationship with God. Jesus modeled the biblical order of worshipping God first, and then serving. After a hard-fought battle in the desert, Jesus uttered the words that drove the devil away, "Away from me, Satan! For it is written: 'Worship the Lord your God, and serve him only'" (Matthew 4:10). Effective cell leaders know that any form of service naturally flows from time spent with the living God. Through acts of selfless service, we extend the Father's love to cell members, to visitors, and to those who don't know Jesus.

My wife is a successful cell leader whose group grew continuously and consistently. Celyce knows that a key to having an effective cell gathering on Friday afternoon is the phone calls she makes Thursday evening. No calls, no shows. Experience has taught her that one additional call often translates into a new member or the return of a "fence sitter."

As you might suspect, the survey shows a relationship between the number of visitors to a group and the number of times a leader multiplies the cell. The more visitors, the more times the leader multiplies the group. However, when compared to visitation of new people and invitation by group members, the number of visitors in the group is secondary. This highlights the importance of the cell leader making contact with visitors right away, as well as cell members taking responsibility for follow-up.

VISITATION OF NEW PEOPLE

The 700 cell-group leaders surveyed were asked how many times a month they contact new people.[1] Each leader was given four options ranging from one to two times per month to eight or more times per month. Suffice it to say, there is a direct correlation between how often cell leaders contact new people and their success in multiplying the group. If leaders contact five to seven new people per month, there is an 80 percent chance that they will multiply the group. When leaders visit one to three people per month, the chances drop to 60 percent. The statistics demonstrate that leaders who visit eight or more new people each month multiply the cell twice as much as those who visit only one or two new people per month. The statistics reveal: Work hard and you'll see the results.

LUIS SALAS

You already met Luis Salas, who multiplied his original cell to 250 cells in just 18 months. Luis goes after potential leaders. He visits new people. Hanging on his bulletin board are lists and more lists of "possible contacts." He meditates on those names day and night. He plans conversations with them and eventually contacts them. He invites them to become cell members and, in time, leaders.

Luis spends the majority of his time now finding, training, and placing leaders. But this same diligent searching characterized his early days as a cell leader. Luis searches out every lead, each new contact. He doesn't wait for opportunity to knock; he knocks and simply opens the door.

GET YOUR FEET WET

Ralph Neighbour Jr. is a practitioner who puts his theory to work among a lost and hurting world. He regularly takes his students to the nearest bar to learn how to befriend those on the other side. One can know all about cell theory, but never reach those in the world.

Wendall Price, the late president of Alliance Theological Seminary in Nyack, New York, is another who practiced what he preached. "Climb down from your ivory towers and visit those in the real world!" he challenged. No wonder churches grew rapidly under his ministry. Study is important, but there comes a time to interact with real people. In fact, the survey of cell leaders indicates that reaching out has a greater impact on cell multiplication than the time a leader spends in lesson preparation.

PRIORITY #1: THE NEW ONES

When Bethany World Prayer Center began transitioning into the cell model four years ago, no one was pressured to join a cell group. The pastors never insisted that all of the members had to be in a group. Rather, the church went after the new people for cell-group members. They concentrated on those without religious backgrounds. Pastor Larry Stockstill states:

> We consistently focus our attention on new converts and visitors: the "growing edge" of the church where the least resistance to relationships is found. Gradually, many of the 'late adopters' have seen the benefits of a cell relationship and are becoming involved. Now about 65 percent of the congregation attend a cell each week.[2]

The ideal in the cell church is that everyone attends both cell and celebration. In reality, there will always be a pool of those who attend only the celebration. Some of these people are visitors; others have attended the church for quite a while. Some will participate in a cell group after one invitation; others require a shove. Aggressively invite all people at the celebration service to the cell: "I'd like to invite you to my cell group on Friday night at 7 p.m. I think you'd really like it. Do you need a ride?" Cell leaders don't need to worry about competition among themselves. Wouldn't it be wonderful if five different cell leaders or interns invited the same visitor?

You've heard that "it's hard to teach an old dog new tricks." Well, it's true in churches, too, so don't be discouraged by the resistance of some. Go after the visitors and the new converts.

These are the people who still have non-Christian contacts to invite to your cell group.

After carefully analyzing growing churches, Herb Miller reaches this conclusion in his book *The Magnetic Church:*

> *No other single factor makes a greater difference in improving annual membership addition than an immediate visit to the home of first-time worshippers. . . . When lay persons make fifteen-minute visits to the homes of first-time worship visitors within thirty-six hours, 85 percent of them return the following week. Make this home visit within seventy-two hours, and 60 percent of them return. Make it seven days later, and 15 percent will return. The pastor making this call, rather than lay persons, cuts each result in half.*[3]

Visiting newcomers right away makes a huge difference. Note how much more impact that visit has if it comes from a lay person rather than from the clergy.

Cell leader, if you want your cell to grow, develop, and multiply, one of the keys is immediate visitation of newcomers. When someone visits your group, plan an immediate follow-up visit, send the person a card, and/or pick up the telephone and call. The saying, "People don't care how much you know until they know how much you care" is true, so care for the newcomers.

The case-study churches have implemented systems so newcomers don't "fall through the cracks." Visitor cards are collected in the church and distributed to the various cell groups, who in turn contact the newcomers. Because of this organized approach to reaching out, many visitors attend a cell. These churches track newcomers to ensure that they receive proper follow-up and care.

At Bethany World Prayer Center, any person who receives Christ or visits the church's celebration service is immediately met by a cell leader. That cell leader then visits the person's home with a gift of bread. The sorting of visitor cards, distribution to cell leaders, and visitation of these newcomers takes place within 24 hours! The cell leaders pray for the visitors and invite them to attend cell.

Love Alive in Honduras receives approximately 110 first-time visitors each month. Some receive Christ during the worship service; others simply want to observe the church. To better care for these visitors, a welcome team takes the names of the visitors at an outside visitor's table. This information is processed, and a cell leader is assigned to personally care for the visitor—by the end of the service! By Monday, the cell leader calls or visits the new person and initiates a four-week follow-up. A member (or leader) of the cell group meets with the person once a week to cover one of the four lessons contained in "Your New Life in Christ," a pamphlet that covers the person's new identity in Christ, spiritual growth, and the importance of the cell group. The last page of the pamphlet contains a final report of the visitation process. From January 1996 to September 1996, 52 percent of the first-time visitors completed the four-week follow-up course!

EXHORTATION IN CELL GROUP TO INVITE FRIENDS

But cell leaders aren't supposed to do it all themselves. Cell evangelism is a team ministry. Cell leaders who mobilize the group to view evangelism as the first priority succeed in cell multiplication. Dale Galloway writes:

> *Although I see all of these purposes as equally important, [he lists evangelism, discipleship, shepherding, and service] a healthy small-group system must always see evangelism as its continuing mission. To keep evangelism thriving in small groups, you must continue to push people out of their comfort zones by encouraging them to call on new people, putting the names of new prospects into their hands, and continually keeping the message of evangelism before them.*[4]

The cell leaders in the case study were asked how many times each month they encourage cell members to invite their friends to the group. Those leaders who consistently encourage cell members to bring friends multiply their groups significantly more than those leaders who do so only occasionally. In fact, leaders who weekly encourage the cell members to invite visitors multiply their groups twice as much as those who do so occasionally or not at all. To be effective, cell leaders mobilize the entire team to invite new people.

One group at Bethany World Prayer Center faithfully met each week but had little growth. One of the cell members who previously attended a group that had multiplied analyzed both groups and then said, "In the other cell group, we received a constant flow of visitors." At that time, another cell was celebrating the birth of a new group. Its cell leader testified that the group went through a dry, difficult period. With only six people, the group did all of the "right things" to win non-Christians and receive visitors, but few visited and fewer stayed. Yet, they kept on trying, praying, and inviting until things finally gelled. Several others began to attend and invited their friends. The mix came together. In that group, four people had come to Christ within the last four months, and at least three of them had come to know Christ in the cell group.

Herb Miller sums up the difference between growing churches and non-growing churches in one word: "invite." He says:

> *70 to 90 percent of persons who join any church in America come through the influence of a friend, of a relative, or of an acquaintance. No amount of theological expression from the pulpit can overcome a lack of invitational expression from the pews.*[5]

Cell leaders must constantly remind the cell members to invite their friends. One cell leader ends her group by asking, "Who are you going to invite next week?" Then she waits for answers. "My mother," says one. "My brother," chimes in another.

And don't be surprised when people who promise to come don't show up. It's common to hear cell leaders say, "I planned desert for four people who failed to show." Welcome to cell leadership. Most cell leaders are familiar with well-intentioned promises by contacts who say they'll visit but fail to follow through. Richard Price and Pat Springer wisely say,

> *Experienced group leaders . . . realize that you usually have to personally invite 25 people for 15 to say they will attend. Of those 15, usually only eight to 10 people will actually show up, and of those, only five to seven will be regular attenders after a month or so.*[6]

Successful cell leaders don't depend on one or two verbal commitments. And instead of getting discouraged, they invite even more people. Consistent personal visitation, repeated calls, and outside group contact result in the visitors who will grow your cell.

YOUR *OIKOS*

Of course, the best people for leaders or cell members to invite are their friends, co-workers, classmates, neighbors and relatives. Ralph Neighbour Jr. has popularized the Greek word, *oikos*, helping the church to understand the importance of reaching our own network of relationships. He writes:

> The word [oikos] is found repeatedly in the New Testament, and is usually translated 'household.' However, it doesn't just refer to family members. Everyone of us have a 'primary group' of friends who relate directly to us through family, work, recreation, hobbies, and neighbors. . . . Newcomers feel very much 'outside' when they visit your group for the first time, unless they have established an oikos connection with one of them. If they are not 'kinned' by the members, they will not stay very long or try very hard to be included before they return to their old friends.[7]

The goal of each cell is to "kin" as many members of our *oikos* as possible. Cells penetrate society through the members' friends, family, and loved ones. Neighbour counsels people to find these web relationships at ". . . your work, your home, your recreational activities, . . . By cultivating a relationship which already existed, you were able to draw them."[8]

On a practical level, those who know us will accept an invitation to attend a cell meeting more readily than strangers. Encourage cell members to love, pray for and invite friends, relatives, coworkers, classmates and neighbors.

David Yonggi Cho writes:

> I have found the only definite way to increase church membership is through personal contact, and personal soul winning. If you know the person, it is better. Since you are personally touching your neighbors, through the cell system, it is far easier to win them to the church.[9]

PRACTICAL SUGGESTIONS

An effective ways to open hearts and attract your *oikos* is through social meetings. Cookouts, sports events, retreats in a mountain cabin, or eating events are non-threatening, non-church environments where non-believers are comfortable.

One cell leader in Ecuador gathered his group at a ranch house on major holidays, or for a sporting event during the week. Cell members invited friends and family to these fun times, and many eventually joined the cell group. To maintain the intimacy in the group and to continue reaching out, this cell gave birth to another cell, and the multiplication process continued.

Part of the "in-reach" that characterizes healthy cells is spending time together outside the regular meeting. And, not surprisingly, there is a close correlation between the number of these outside meetings and the number of times cell leaders multiply their groups. The surveyed cell leaders were asked how many times a month their group meets for social occasions outside of the regular cell group meeting. Their answers: 27 percent, zero times; 30 percent, once; 19 percent, two or three; 18 percent, four or five; and 5 percent, six or more times. Those who gather six or more times a month for social meetings multiply their group twice as much as those who meet never or only once.

This is one area that the statistical study makes very clear. Having fun together is magnetic for cell members. Leaders who unite their cell members outside the regular meeting multiply their groups more rapidly. This seems like an obvious truth, but it requires lots of planning and prayer.

Another common way to attract non-Christians is to occasionally transform the normal cell meeting into an evangelistic event. These "seeker-sensitive" meetings focus on non-Christians. Group members think like non-Christians when planning the ice-breaker, the lesson, the refreshments, and even the prayer and worship time. The success of the "seeker-sensitive" cell depends on every member inviting as many non-Christian friends as possible, followed with diligent prayer.

Also try evangelistic dinners, social events, cookouts, and parties. Jesus was always eating with people—often in their homes. The early church shared meals in the home. Food, a relaxed atmosphere, and getting to know new people make a great combination. Non-Christians like informal, free-flowing gatherings where they're not the center of attention.

Show portions of a secular video and follow it with discussion. One cell invited non-Christians to watch a portion of "Schindler's List" (about the Jewish Holocaust). After 15 minutes of video, the group shared about the "meaning of life" that naturally flowed from the movie.

Moving the cell from house to house is another excellent way to attract visitors. When a cell member hosts the meeting in his or her home, that member's friends and family are more likely to attend. After all, many of these people have already visited the home, thus eliminating one barrier—fear of the unknown.

At your next cell meeting, pass out index cards and ask each member to write the names of people they could invite to the group. Then ask them to pray for those people every day. At Bethany World Prayer Center, each cell records the names of potential visitors on a mini-white board and uses that as a prayer list ever since Pastor Larry Stockstill observed this method in one cell he visited.

The potential to attract visitors through specialized cell outreach is enormous. Remember, however, that pragmatism is the key. Do what works for you. The bottom line is whether the event actually attracts visitors. If so, use that vehicle repeatedly until it loses its effectiveness. Then try something else.

In addition to growing your group and God's kingdom, visitors refresh cell ministry. Their questions enlighten otherwise dull, boring meetings. They don't necessarily give "acceptable" answers or ask "polite" questions. Once a visitor to a cell asked the most sincere, heartfelt questions concerning her struggles in marriage. The cell members immediately responded to her need with practical, biblical answers. The excitement of meeting practical needs flowed through that small group, and no one was in a hurry to leave. Such is cell life. It's meant to meet the deepest needs and touch hurts and wounds. Visitors remind long-term members of a lost, hurting world. Effective cells do what it takes to assure a constant flow of visitors by seeking new people and constantly inviting non-Christians.

8

REACH OUT
AS A TEAM

L uke 5:1-7 is the story about Jesus and a great catch of fish. The disciples had fished all night and caught nothing. But at Jesus' command, they cast out their nets once again. We read in verses 6 & 7, "When they had done so, they caught such a large number of fish that their nets began to break. So they signaled their *partners* in the other boat to come and help them, and they came and filled both boats so full that they began to sink." Then in verse 10, it states that Simon and his *partners*, James and John, were astonished at the catch.

PARTNERSHIP IN GROUP EVANGELISM

In the first reference to Peter's partners, a technical term for a business partner is used. But in verse 10, Luke uses a different Greek word for partners, one that means those who have *koinonia* fellowship. Peter and his partners worked together to haul in the huge catch. As they would work together to catch men, their fellowship would take on a new and much deeper sharing. Likewise, in cell ministry, the best fellowship occurs in the process of evangelizing.

Group outreach is the heartbeat of cell ministry. Bill Mangham, my close associate in Ecuador, often experienced this type of *koinonia* fellowship in his cells. The entire group planned outreach events on a regular basis. Once they used the story of Zacchaeus, the tax collector whom Jesus transformed (Luke 19:1-10), for their cell lesson. Everyone helped plan the cell meeting: one brought refreshments; another prepared the ice-breaker; Bill's wife, Ann, took care of the house and provided some food; everyone in the group prayed over their *oikos* relationships (family, friends, work associates) and then actively invited those whom Jesus brought to mind. Four non-Christians attended the group for the first time that night. The cell reached out to the newcomers and made them feel like family. After the lesson, Bill invited everyone to meet Jesus in the quiet of their own hearts. No one knew who had accepted Jesus until the refreshment time afterward. René, a member of the cell, asked the couple he invited what they thought about the lesson. They told him that they had accepted Jesus during the prayer time. Jesus transformed this couple. They became faithful members of the cell group and eventually started attending the celebration services as well.

What happened in Bill Mangham's cell group is not unique. Yet most evangelistic training in the United States concentrates on the individual. Individuals receive instruction on how to share the gospel at work, home, or school. Individuals experience the joys of winning people to Christ and the agony of rejection.

In contrast, cell evangelism is a shared experience. Everyone gets involved—from the person who invites the guests, to the one who provides refreshments, to the one who leads the discussion. The team plans, strategizes, and finds new contacts together. Dale Galloway writes, "Once the list [of invitees] is built, the team begins to pray the prospect list, then to work it—making phone calls and home visitations. This responsibility can be shared with others in the small group."[1]

Each member is trained in how to share the faith, and then cell groups work together to haul in the large catch of fish. The clear-cut goal of the group is to grow to the point of multiplication.

Imagine soldiers fighting a battle together, with the common goal of conquering the enemy. Although the clear focus is defeating the enemy and winning the war, some close fellowship takes place in the process. We've all heard stories about the enduring bonds of friendship among military veterans. Perhaps it's because in life and death situations, a mutual dependency develops which results in close, lasting fellowship. As cell members unite to fight the evil forces of this world and reach the lost for Christ, close and intimate fellowship takes place.

David Yonggi Cho says that only those with the gift of evangelism can successfully lead a cell group.[2] This would be true only if the cell leader was personally responsible for bringing all new members into the cell group. Research at these eight large cell churches shows that successful cell growth is a team experience. The leader mobilizes the troops to do the work of the ministry (Ephesians 4:12). Michael C. Mack refers to this team effort in his book *The Synergy Church*. He writes:

> *The synergy of the small group is an especially positive factor in the witness of the group. Evangelism is best when it is a team, not an individual, effort. The various gifts of members allow the group to reach lost people in a way no individual could. When all the members see themselves as witnesses wherever they are—in the offices, factories, neighborhoods, schools, hospitals, stores— the entire group can have a tremendous impact, especially when each member is praying for and encouraging everyone else.[3]*

As stated earlier, the survey of cell leaders did not pinpoint any one particular spiritual gift among those leaders who multiply their group. They operate in their own area of giftedness, but they know how to harness and unify the gifts of everyone in the group to do the work of the ministry.

NET FISHING VS. HOOK FISHING

The tools of the fisherman—the net and the fishing pole—best illustrate small-group evangelism. Cell-group evangelism uses the net to catch fish. In every sense of the word, it is *group* evangelism. Everyone participates. Larry Stockstill of Bethany World Prayer Center describes it this way:

> *The old paradigm of 'hook fishing' is being replaced by teams of believers who have entered into partnership ('community') for the purpose of reaching souls together. . . . Jesus used the 'partnership' of net fishing to illustrate the greatest principle of evangelism: our productivity is far greater together than alone.[4]*

Likewise, Cho credits the growth of his 700,000+ church to the net fishing that takes place in the cell groups.[5] He highlights his methodology of cell group evangelism by saying:

Our cell group system is a net for our Christians to cast. Instead of a pastor fishing for one fish at a time, organized believers form nets to gather hundreds and thousands of fish. A pastor should never try to fish with a single rod but should organize believers into the 'nets' of a cell system.[6]

Although one might not agree with everything that David Cho says and does, the fact that he has 700,000+ members in his church stirs all those interested in church growth to listen attentively. Effective evangelism and discipleship through cell groups is not only a possibility; it's a serious reality.

GROUP EVANGELISM THROUGH EDIFICATION

Christ told his disciples that their love would draw the world to Himself. More than just a prayer of unity, Christ's prayer for His disciples in John 17 is a call to evangelism. Jesus says:

My prayer is not for them alone. I pray also for those who will believe in me through their message, that all of them may be one, Father, just as you are in me and I am in you. May they also be in us so that the world may believe that you have sent me. I in them and you in me. May they be brought to complete unity to let the world know that you sent me and have loved them even as you have loved me (vv. 20-21, 23).

To many, unity and evangelism mix as well as oil and water. They appear to be opposites that repel each other. Christ tells us, however, that unity among believers attracts non-Christians to God. Peter writes, "Above all, love each other deeply, because love covers over a multitude of sins" (1 Peter 4:8). The adjective "deeply" in this verse literally means "stretch out." It denotes the tense muscle activity of an athlete in the midst of a race. As believers stretch out their love, acceptance, and forgiveness to other members of the cell, the world sees and then believes that Jesus Christ lives. Several veterans of small-group ministry team up to write:

And that is the purpose of all this—of caring for one another . . . so that the world will know that Jesus Christ is Lord. That's why the church exists in the first place. The ultimate goal of the small group is to expose people who don't know Jesus Christ to His love. We have small groups so the world can see Christ fleshed out. It's our way of taking Christ to the world.[7]

GROUP EVANGELISM THROUGH FRIENDSHIP

Few non-Christians enter a church community "cold turkey." They don't wake up one Sunday and decide to attend church. Those who do receive this kind of "jolt" to attend church normally don't stay, because they don't have friends in the church. Church-growth studies reveal that friendship is one of the key links to sustained church growth. Win Arn suggests that a person must develop at least six key friendships in a church to continue attending.[8]

The cell church is uniquely positioned to provide such friendships. The cell becomes a second family to many. In the cell, these family relationships are often established before the non-Christian attends the church's large celebration service. Dale Galloway writes, "Many people who will not attend a church because it is too threatening, will come to a home meeting."[9] Later, these same non-Christians will enter the church at the side of a friend they've met in the cell group. Cho writes,

I tell my cell leaders, 'Don't tell people about Jesus Christ right away when you meet them. First visit them and become their friend, supply their needs and love them.' Right away the neighbors will feel the Christian love and will say, 'Why are you doing this?' They can answer, 'We belong to Yoido Full Gospel Church, and have our own cell group here, and we love you. Why don't you come and attend one of our meetings?' So they come and are converted.[10]

Cell ministry effectively blends the decision to follow Christ and discipleship. A "built-in" follow-up system is already in place through the cells. Those converted in the cell will enter the larger church with new family members.

GROUP EVANGELISM THROUGH HONEST TRANSPARENCY

How do you naturally present the gospel to a non-Christian? Why can we as believers talk about sports, politics, work and family at great length, but freeze up when we talk about our faith? Even though many of us have memorized ways to present the gospel, these often lack the natural link to the non-Christian's heart. Small-group evangelism provides this missing link.

Richard Peace, professor of evangelism at Fuller Theological Seminary, wrote a book entitled *Small Group Evangelism* that recently has been reprinted.[11] Peace believes a non-Christian can manifest deep, personal needs and find the healing touch of Christ in a small group. He writes:

> In a successful small group, love, acceptance and fellowship flow in unusual measure. This is the ideal situation in which to hear about the kingdom of God. In this context, the 'facts of the gospel' come through not as cold proposition but as living truths visible in the lives of others. In such an atmosphere, a person is irresistibly drawn to Christ by his gracious presence.[12]

As Peace points out, evangelism in the small group is a natural process. Non-Christians can ask questions, share doubt, and talk about their own spiritual journey. Meanwhile, Christ-like cell members share their testimonies while presenting a clear, non-comprising gospel message. Peace notes, "Our failure to be honest is probably the greatest hindrance to easy and natural conversational witness."[13] Honesty and transparency abound in a healthy cell group.

Each cell member should receive training about how to present the eternal facts of the gospel. But evangelism in a small group does not emphasize a canned, memorized approach. The gospel is not preached but shared in a loving, natural manner.

Remember that Wesley's cell group model, the class meeting, was not a highly organized event. Although they met only for one hour, the main event was "reporting on your soul."[14] The meeting was built upon sharing personal experiences of the past week. Everyone was expected ". . . to speak freely and plainly about every subject from their own temptations to plans for establishing a new cottage meeting or visiting the distressed."[15] In other words, these groups emphasized transparency. Within this framework of "open sharing," many were converted. The hearts of sinners melted as they interacted with "saved sinners." Jesus Christ made all the difference.

Transparent sharing, love, and acceptance reveal to non-Christians that believers are indeed not perfect—just forgiven. One of Satan's chief tactics is legalistic deception, trying to convince people that God requires unreachable standards and that only "good" people enter heaven. Small-group evangelism corrects that misconception. Open sharing gives unbelievers a new sense of hope as they realize that Christians have weaknesses and struggles, too. The difference is that Christians place their sin and struggles at the foot of the cross of Jesus.

GUIDING THE GROUP INTO DEEPER LEVELS OF COMMUNICATION

The leader must share personal struggles. If the leader is prone to impress others by recounting only the "victories," cell members will do likewise. David Hocking exhorts group leaders to, "Learn to admit your mistakes in the presence of the group and to apologize sincerely when things go wrong or do not turn out the way you expected. Admitting failure in the midst of success is a key to good leadership. Learn to be open and honest before others. They'll love you for it (or at least fall over backwards out of shock!)."[16]

The cell leader must model good listening skills. Stephen Covey hits on a common flaw when he says that most people do not listen to understand; they listen to answer. While one is talking, the other is preparing a reply.[17] Members know the leader is not listening if he or she is rustling through notes in preparation for the next question, while a cell member answers the last question the leader asked. When members sense that the leader is not listening, they will hesitate to openly share the next time.

Avoid critiquing when someone shares personal truth. If the cell leader criticizes a response, others will be more hesitant to respond. There is always a way to respond positively, even if someone's answer is wrong.

The meeting does not have to be "feeling oriented," but it does need honest, open communication. During the church's celebration time, it's OK to be anonymous and lost in the crowd, because close communication in the cell places a "face" on that lost person in the crowd and opens the door for individual ministry. It's not OK, however, to try to remain lost in the small group. At first, sharing in the group might cover the latest weather or sports. Over time, however, the cell leader directs the conversation to deeper levels. Judy Hamlin outlines the various levels of communication this way:

1. Level One: Climate, family
2. Level Two: Information or facts
3. Level Three: Ideas and opinions
4. Level Four: Feelings
5. Level Five: Sharing what is truly happening in our lives

She then gives the following illustration about the natural progression in communication from the superficial to the intimate.[18]

LEVEL I	LEVEL II	LEVEL III & IV	LEVEL V
Mary: Hi Rebecca: How was the weather in Florida? Rebecca: Most of the time it was just great. Mary: You must have had a great time.	Rebecca: Yes, I did, but you know I was thinking about the famine in Ethiopia, and it really made me think about the serious problems in the world. Do you think much about the fact that many people die for lack of food?	Mary: Yes, for me it is a very sad situation. When I see all the hungry people on television, it really makes me sad. Especially because we're not doing more to the change the situation.	Rebecca: For me, the famine is not something that I just see on television. My sister became anorexic. Last month, she died.

Table 4. Levels of Communication

86

The cell group is an effective way to reach deeply into the heart of non-Christian men and women. It is evangelism that is caught and taught. It is show-and-tell evangelism, rather than only propositional truth. The New Testament church was born, grew, and prospered in and through small-group evangelism. God is calling His church once again to this exciting method of outreach. Along with honest, open sharing, small groups must actively reach out to the community around them. Let's look at some examples of how cells actively and aggressively reach their communities through pro-active group evangelism.

LOVE ALIVE CHURCH

This cell church in Honduras works on the zone level to plan evangelistic activities, and each cell in the zone participates. The zone might present a Christian movie, a special speaker, or some type of servant evangelism, depending on the particular zone. Christian movies and door-to-door evangelism are popular in the poorer areas of Tegucigalpa, while the higher-income areas demand more creative methods.

Each cell is encouraged to reach its neighborhood for the zone-level events, and for special occasions that the cell itself sponsors. Some groups might create special cards inviting neighborhood mothers to a Mother's Day celebration. Or the cell might plan a special dinner and invite those living in the neighborhood. Another favorite at Love Alive is an outdoor activity featuring singing and a speaker.

Group evangelism intensifies before the birth of a new cell and targets the area in which the new group will meet. The new leadership team, members from the mother group, and the area supervisor evangelize the neighborhood together.

FAITH COMMUNITY BAPTIST CHURCH

Two bedrock truths make up the "cell manifesto" at Faith Community Baptist Church in Singapore—ministry to one another, and multiplication.[19] Cell members are constantly reminded to reach their *oikos*—their extended web of close relationships. Cells are encouraged to hold a social event every six weeks to attract non-Christians.

The current evangelistic thrust occurs through so-called "harvest events." They used to happen only in FCBC's large celebration gatherings, but harvest events also take place within the cell now. "TGIF" ("Thank God It's Friday") is a Good Friday outreach that focuses each cell on inviting non-Christian friends to a carefully planned, seeker-sensitive meeting. Communion is served, and a portion of the *Jesus* film is shown. Another harvest event within the cell is "Come Celebrate Christmas!" and takes place Christmas Eve or Christmas Day. A large, celebration-type harvest event takes place in August, usually a music concert. Through events like these, FCBC harvested almost 3,000 souls in 1996.

RALPH NEIGHBOUR'S MODEL

Ralph Neighbour Jr.'s materials teach cell groups to distinguish "Type A" unbelievers who are fairly open to Christian faith from "Type B" unbelievers who ". . . are not searching for Jesus Christ, and show no interest in Bible study or other Christian activities."[20] For the "Type B" unbelievers, Neighbour designed a "non-Christian type" group called Share Groups. These do not replace the cell group but rather serve as an extension of it. Believers who participate in Share Groups have the dual responsibility of attending their normal cell group as well as the separate Share Group. Neighbour writes, "This group should be free, informal, and spontaneous. . . . It's important for all Share Group members to feel they can be themselves."[21] Share Groups allow cell groups to reach hard-core unbelievers who are not yet open to the gospel but who are open to friendships.

A FEW PROVEN GROUP EVANGELISM IDEAS

- Plan a "friendship dinner" instead of the normal cell meeting and invite non-Christian friends.

- During a cell meeting, watch an evangelistic video instead of having a Bible-based lesson.

- Place a empty chair in the cell meeting and have the members pray for the next person who will fill it.

- Prepare a special outreach to one segment of society, such as police officers or teachers (Bethany World Prayer Center uses this approach with great success).

- Plan a picnic for the purpose of inviting friends.

- Plan short skits for outdoor evangelism.

- Have members of the group dress up as clowns to attract a crowd while others share Christ.

9

EVANGELIZE BY
MEETING NEEDS

In the New Testament period, Peter writes to the house churches, "Above all, love each other deeply, because love covers over a multitude of sins. Offer hospitality to one another without grumbling" (1 Peter 4:8-9). Hospitality was an essential feature in the early church (Matthew 25: 35; Romans 12:13; 16; 3-5a; 1 Thessalonians 3:2). Since there were no church buildings, Christian homes were converted into both the local church—and, often, into the local inn. Traveling preachers and missionaries stayed in believers' homes. "Priscilla and Aquila were accustomed to extending the hospitality of their home to such groups in the successive cities where they lived—e.g. in Ephesus (1 Corinthians 16:19) and Rome (Romans 16:5)."[1]

New Testament hospitality in the context of the home is an often overlooked evangelistic tool. Meeting people's needs in the context of the home cell edifies the saints and draws non-Christians to the Savior. Most non-Christians will "hear" our actions before listening to our words.

Take, for example, the story of a pregnant, single woman named Maria, who began attending my wife's cell group in Ecuador. Maria's boyfriend had deserted her, and she suddenly faced life poor and alone. The cell group became a family to her, and they prepared for the baby as though it were their own. They even gave Maria a baby shower at one of the cell meetings. When Maria went into labor, a cell member drove her to the hospital. Another took her and the baby home, and the cell members provided meals for her for over one week.

Maria experienced God's unconditional love through the

group. She desired the Savior that they demonstrated even before the gospel was formally presented to her. Receiving Christ was a logical decision for Maria, since God's love was shown to her in very practical ways just when she needed it most. She and her baby attended the cell group in the following weeks, and Maria received Jesus Christ as her Lord and Savior.

David Cho is quick to point out that "meeting practical needs" is the reason for his church's indisputable success in attracting new people. The cell leaders and members are encouraged to "find a need and meet it."[2] Cell members are instructed to go into the "highways and byways" and invite all who are needy. After all, these are the people who benefit most from the cell group. In a 1993 interview with Carl George, Cho explained his strategy of winning the lost through meeting practical needs:

> We have 50,000 cell groups and each group will love two people to Christ within the next year. They select someone who's not a Christian, whom they can pray for, love, and serve. They bring meals, help sweep out the person's store—whatever it takes to show they really care for them. . . . After three or four months of such love, the hardest soul softens up and surrenders to Christ.[3]

Through the loving outreach of the cell, these people soon discover the answer to their life's dilemmas in Jesus Christ.

Knowing each other and sharing needs are primary goals of cell groups. In this atmosphere of warmth and love, cell members discover and then meet individual needs. Cells practicing New Testament hospitality will remember the words of the apostle John, "If anyone has material possessions and sees his brother in need but has no pity on him, how can the love of God be in him? Dear children, let us not love in words or tongue but with actions and in truth" (1 John 3:17-18). Ron Nicholas gives a personal example,

> When my car failed to start once in ten-below-zero winter weather, Steve and Cathy (a couple in our Koinonia group at church) loaned me their brand new car so that I could drive to work. When my wife, Jill, returned from the hospital with our new twin girls, we enjoyed several meals brought in by members

of the same small group. We cried together when one member told
of a car accident and problems at work. We all feel the pain when
a couple's child is in the hospital.[4]

Effective, growing small groups do more than pray. They meet needs in practical ways.

EVANGELISM THROUGH COMMUNITY OUTREACH

Cincinnati Vineyard Community Church is adopting a significant new norm for their small groups. Every four to six weeks, each group engages in "servant evangelism," an outreach to non-Christians.[5] Pastor David Stiles explained in 1995 that 15 percent of the church's finances are used for kindness ministries: purchasing and changing light bulbs for people, raking leaves, offering cold drinks to commuters on summer afternoon, etc. No strings or formal gospel presentations are attached, Stiles says, but each recipient of kindness is given an informational card about the church. Many people attend the church and cell groups as a result.

Church of the Savior in Washington, D.C., has practiced social outreach for many years. The five to 12 people in each cell group pray, study and worship together, and these mission groups are conscious of their social responsibility to those outside the group. Ronald J. Sider explains:

The goal of many of the mission groups is liberation for the poor.
Members of the mission group called Jubilee Housing have
renovated deteriorating housing in inner-city Washington.
Along with other mission groups . . . they are bringing hope of
genuine change to hundreds of people in the inner city.[6]

Living Word Community Church in Philadelphia is another example of practical love in action. In 1970, the church reorganized around home cell groups. The church radically changed in numerical expansion and in community living. Sider writes:

Members of home meetings have dug into savings and stocks to
provide interest-free loans for two families who purchased house

trailers for homes. When members went to sign the papers for an interest-free mortgage for another family's house, secular folk present for the transfer were totally perplexed![7]

A more recent, dynamic example is occurring at Faith Community Baptist Church. FCBC reaches out to meet the physical needs of the Singaporeans through day-care centers, after-school clubs, centers for the handicapped, diabetic support groups, and legal counseling.[8] Cell members are encouraged to participate both individually and at a larger level (cell or zone) in the social ministries of Touch Community Services. Volunteers from the cell groups often come along side staff members to help in practical ways, as well as to share their faith. The range and depth of ministry at Touch Community Service Center is staggering.

In the book *Good Things Happen in Small Groups* the suggestion is made,

Each small group could care for one shut-in from the church. You can send cards on birthdays and special occasions, provide a visit at least monthly, bring a meal and eat with them, bring families (children included) when appropriate. If there are many shut-ins in your church, each family unit could take one as their care-burden.[9]

Other ideas: a particular cell group might decide to reach out to the community by visiting a retirement home, ministering to street kids, or helping out in an orphanage. The cell group offers a unique, effective way to reach deeply into the heart of non-Christians. This is show-and-tell evangelism, rather than only propositional truth. The New Testament church was born, grew and prospered through small-group evangelism. God is calling His Church back once again to this exciting method of outreach.

10

PREPARE FOR A SMOOTH DELIVERY

My wife and I were emotionally "pumped up" for the birth of our first child. Everyone told us that the first birth would be the most intense, both physically and emotionally. They were right. With this counsel in mind, we spent hours practicing breathing techniques and learning about the birth process. We were living in Ecuador and were blessed to receive the help of a midwife whose husband worked at the U.S. embassy. She sacrificed hours to teach us about the process and was at our side when Sarah was born in Quito. The midwife's practical tips helped remove our fear of the unknown.

Similarly, giving birth to a cell group requires detailed planning and preparation. Having some practical knowledge about cell development and multiplication gives you confidence to successfully birth a new group. Granted, an element of mystery and unexplainable circumstances always remains, but mastering certain techniques saves needless pain and confusion.

SPECIAL CONSIDERATIONS

Jesus says in John 16:21-22, "A woman giving birth to a child has pain because her time has come; but when her baby is born she forgets the anguish because of her joy that a child is born into the world." Childbirth is a painful experience, as my wife can thrice testify. Yet, after the agonizing experience of the first two, she was more than ready to give birth to another. For my wife, the joy of having and holding her child by far exceeded the pain of childbirth. Floyd L. Schwanz says, "Contractions can be expected and should not come as a surprise. Some mothers have very slight discomfort; for others it is severe and very painful. So it is with birthing groups. But no matter what has been experienced, the new life is cause for celebration."[1]

Many cells never give birth. Though the following list is by no means exhaustive, my cell experience and research have surfaced three common reasons for a cell not giving birth.

1) Group members become too comfortable with each other. They cling tightly to their relationships and do not want to let go, even if it means that new people would be won into the Kingdom. This is the church-growth disease *koinonitus*, which is caused by over-emphasizing Christian fellowship and overlooking Christ's commission to reach those who don't know Him. Indeed, cell members are encouraged to develop intimate relationships, but not to the point of excluding others. Remind them that even if they leave the cell to plant another group, they can still contact friends in their former cell. In fact, the mother and daughter cells might reunite on occasion to celebrate the greater goal of evangelism and church growth.

2) Members don't know the great joy that accompanies giving birth to a new cell, contributing to the growth of the church, and growing Christ's kingdom. Explanation alone cannot solve this dilemma. This joy must be experienced.

3) After experiencing the beauty of God's Spirit moving in the small group, there is a fear that the next group will fall short. People have an often unexpressed concern that the new group could not possibly be as anointed as the present one. It's the age-old problem of believing that the bygone days are somehow superior to the present or future. Solomon addresses it: "Do not say, 'Why were the old days better than these?' For it is not wise to ask such questions" (Ecclesiastes 7:10). To overcome this tendency, cell leaders and members must continually be reminded that the Spirit of God will make the next cell group just as

special as the present one. The words of Ralph Neighbour Jr. should be heeded, "The beauty of the cell church continues even when the group gives birth because the power of the Spirit continues to work in the life of the new group."[2]

PROMOTION OF NEW CELLS

Cell leaders and interns who have multiplied their cell groups should be highly esteemed before the congregation.[3] Dale Galloway talks about the importance of motivating your cell leaders by giving them attention, appreciation and affirmation,[4] and this is especially true of those who have birthed a daughter cell.

KNOW WHEN TO MULTIPLY

And just how do you know when it's time to multiply your cell group? Is there any specific size a group much reach beforehand?

Unless small groups remain small, they lose their effectiveness and their ability to care for the needs of each member. Growth in size normally excludes growth in intimacy, and this is the most compelling reason to multiply. As the size of a small group increases, there is a direct decrease of equally distributed participation. In other words, as the small-group size increases, there is a growing difference in the percentage of remarks made by the most active person and by the least active person.[5]

From a practical standpoint, therefore, cell groups must multiply to maintain intimacy among members while continuing to reach out to non-Christians. Each cell's emphasis on evangelism and on non-believers joining the group spurs the cell's growth. This continual growth compels the cell to multiply to remain effective.

Cell church experts agree that a group must be small enough for all members to freely contribute and share personal needs. They don't agree, however, on what that means in exact numbers. Many believe that the perfect size lies between eight and 12 people. Dale Galloway said, "The ideal number for good group dynamics and for caring and dialogue is somewhere between eight and 12. Participation is much greater when you stay within those numbers."[6] John Mallison, a veteran small-group practitioner, writes, "Twelve not only sets the upper limit for meaningful relationships, but provides a non-threatening situation for those who are new to small group experiences. . . . It is significant that Jesus chose 12 men to be in his group."[7]

On the other hand, Carl George sets the number at 10. He is more emphatic that this is the perfect size for a cell group because it is ". . . the time-tested, scientifically validated size that allows for optimal communication."[8] Perhaps a bit dogmatic, George's point is well worth noting. He believes that a group must remain small in order for a leader to give quality pastoral care.

The experience of Love Alive Church in Tegucigalpa, Honduras, supports an optimal number of 10. For a long time, this church waited until a group had 15 people before multiplying. They saw, however, that it was difficult for a group to maintain an average of 15 people over a long period of time. So a few years ago, the leadership decided that any group averaging 10 people on a regular basis would be a candidate for multiplication. Dixie Rosales, the church's cell director, reports that the change helped revolutionize small-group multiplication in the church. Many more groups qualify for multiplication now, and the proliferation of cells is spreading more rapidly throughout Love Alive Church.

A Variety of Ways to Multiply

Cell leaders need to prayerfully weigh some options before multiplying a group. Let's look at an overview of the two approaches—cell planting and cell multiplication—and at the variations within each.

CELL PLANTING

With cell planting, a member of an existing group starts his or her own cell from scratch. Planters normally launch a cell by gathering their oikos members (friends, family, work contacts) into a new cell group. The planter continues to have a relationship with the mother group, or at least with the group's leader. Cell planting is the primary style of group multiplication at the International Charismatic Mission in Bogota, Colombia, and at the Living Water Church in Lima, Peru. Bethany World Prayer Center in Louisiana also now emphasizes this method.

CELL MULTIPLICATION

In the so-called "mother-daughter" multiplication approach, an existing cell group oversees the creation of a daughter group by providing people, leadership, and a measure of personal care to help support it. A group is formed from within the mother cell and is sent to form a daughter cell. This is the traditional, most frequently used method of cell multiplication. Most churches in my case study concentrated on this method, with only occasional ventures into cell planting.

Traditionally, the mother cell forms a new nucleus consisting of the new leader, the new intern, and a few members from the mother cell. Of the eight churches I studied, six also included a treasurer (responsible for the cell offering) on the new team. Note that the leader of this team probably served as the mother cell's intern. Whether the intern stays in the original group or launches out to start a new group depends on that person's maturity and leadership level.

The second most common variation of the mother-daughter approach is for the cell leader to launch out with several members of the mother cell. In this scenario, the cell intern then takes the helm of the mother cell. Track records at many churches worldwide show that both of these variations work well.

FORM NEW GROUPS WITHOUT DESTROYING THEM

Successful cell multiplication is an art. The leader must exercise great care and sensitivity in forming the new group, or run the risk of alienating the members. Donald McGavran makes the revolutionary claim that the greatest barriers to conversion are social rather than theological,[9] and this often holds true in cell evangelism. It's always better to form new groups according to natural *oikos* relationships. Why alienate a non-Christian by insisting that he or she form part of a new group of strangers?

MULTIPLY ALONG RELATIONAL LINES

Again, those people who have formed natural links to each other should stay together. If someone has invited a visitor, he or she will go with the invitee. Perhaps the reflection of a district pastor in Cho's church will be helpful,

> *As much as possible, we divide groups based on natural networks. For example, if the assistant in that group brought two other cell members to the Lord, then that individual will split off with those members to start a new group. If there are no natural networks, then we divide the groups based on geography.''*[10]

Bob Logan adds,

> *A group ripped asunder without regard for the naturally occurring segments or affinity clusters within the group will make a big mess. If you split a group by arbitrarily counting off, or in this culture, even by using geographical boundaries or some means other than affinity clusters, you may end up with many injured group members. However, if you identify naturally occurring affinity or relational clusters within your group, plant a leader for each (or watch to see what leader naturally emerges to the top of each), and then divide the group by these clusters, the result will be much more beneficial. To encourage the formation of these clusters, start early in the group's life to experiment with different cluster compositions. Perhaps allow your members to divide by their own devices into groups or three, four, or five members. Note who gravitated to whom, and who took leadership. Try this for three or four weeks to see if any specific clusters are gelling.*[11]

The wise cell leader will continually analyze natural friendship links. When the time comes to give birth, the leader's discernment will prove very helpful.

Second, if natural links can't be established, the more mature Christian believers accompany the intern and the newcomers or less mature stay with the original cell leader.

Before the birth occurs, the new group's members should meet together by themselves. For example, it's a good idea for this nucleus to gather with the mother cell for the "normal" cell meeting. After the entire group worships together, the new nucleus and intern separate into a different part of the home for discussion, planning, and prayer. This helps ease the two groups into their separate identities, and to experience what their cells will be like after they multiply. This also forges solid links for the new group.[12]

BEGIN WITH A PARTY

Ecuadorians love to celebrate. When my wife gave birth to our daughters, we received a constant barrage of visitors and well-wishers. Likewise, the birth of a new cell group is a joyous occasion. Celebrate the new birth! Invite as many people as possible. Some will stay and join to strengthen the new group. Bethany World Prayer Center celebrates cell multiplication with parties. Often the entire cell will go to a park and have a big barbecue.

I attended a "birthday celebration"—complete with a birthday cake—for a new cell at Bethany. What a joyous occasion! We sang, heard testimonies, feasted, and fervently prayed for the new daughter. The top leadership connected with the mother cell testified, prayed, and commissioned the new daughter. The leader of the cell reflected back to harder days when only a handful attended. But at the birthday party, all could see God's sovereign hand. Recognizing a new birth in this way provides the "jump start" necessary for the new group to run well. It also creates an opportunity to encourage and pray for the new cell leadership.

LENGTH OF TIME TO MULTIPLY

In many of the most rapidly growing cell churches around the world, it takes an individual cell about six months to multiply.[13] Neighbour writes,

Long years of experience with groups has verified that they stagnate after a certain period. People draw from one another for the first six months; after that, they tend to 'coast' along together. For that reason, each Shepherd Group will be expected to multiply naturally after six months or be restructured.[14]

My research of the five Latin America countries shows that a cell multiplies in exactly six months. But that time swells to an average of nearly nine months when the Singapore and Korea statistics are included, because those churches multiply cells in closer to 18 months. Floyd L. Schwanz reaches these conclusions:

Through the years, we have noticed that the average is about 6 months. Some groups will be ready to birth a new group in 3 or 4 months, but some will need 9 to 12 months to raise up leaders who can take new responsibility in another circle of love. It is not the size of the group that determines its ability to multiply; it is the health.[15]

WILL YOU CLOSE CELLS THAT DON'T MULTIPLY?

Whether cell groups should be allowed to continue indefinitely without multiplying is a very hot topic, with advocates on both sides.

Cells that fail to multiply don't face a closure date in Cho's church or in the five Latin American churches that I studied. In fact, cell pastors in Colombia and El Salvador said it was a "sin" to close a group. These churches in Latin America, as well as Yoido Full Gospel, keep cells open as long as possible. They will, however, make drastic adjustments—including changing leaders and/or members—to multiply groups.

The other side has a number of advocates as well. Faith Community Baptist Church in Singapore teaches cell interns,

Generally, the life span of any Cell should be between six to nine months. We have discovered that any Cell which does not multiply after about 12 months will usually stagnate, lose its life or dynamism and eventually die. Every Cell should have an ending of some sort, and each member should realize this from the beginning. Multiplication is a time of celebration. The Leader must help to make multiplication a pleasant occasion for everyone.[16]

Pastor David Tan of First Baptist Church in Modesto, California, once said, "Everything that has life has a cycle. As you study the cell, it must give life. If you keep a cell that is not multiplying, it will die. The choice is life and death." At First Baptist, cells have one year to multiply; after that, they are integrated into existing cells. Win Arn finds that groups meeting for more than one year without multiplying have only a 50 percent chance of doing so in the future.[17]

ADVANTAGES OF CLOSING CELLS

- The cell cannot stagnate and become ingrown. Members are given new vision as they integrate into dynamic, multiplying cells.
- The cell begins with the goal of multiplication.
- Leaders are less likely to "burn out," and members do not feel the pressure of a life-long commitment. There is a way out.
- Existing cells receive additional members.

DISADVANTAGES OF CLOSING CELLS

- Leaders and members often have a sense of failure when a group is asked to close.
- Pressure is placed upon cell leadership and cell membership to multiply or fail.
- Groups that close can match groups that open so there is no net growth.

When a cell group becomes cancerous and dysfunctional, closure is the best policy. But such decisions should stay within the upper circles of cell leadership. It's unwise to teach or promote cell closure ("multiply or close") to cell leaders and interns, because this places undo pressure on the cell leader and cell group. It's hard enough for a lay person to multiply a cell without the added burden of "possible failure." While some can handle this kind of pressure, others will avoid cell leadership because of it, thus preventing future leaders from volunteering. For example, cells in one church I visited were stagnating and failing to attract new leadership, and several cell leaders attributed this pattern to the possibility of cell closure. While closure may be necessary at times, this should not be the norm. And certainly no cell should be closed before every possible avenue to multiply the group has been exhausted.

11

UNDERSTAND
CELL PLANTING

C ell planting has always existed in the cell church. It's now at the forefront of cell thinking, due largely to the influence of the International Charismatic Mission in Bogota, Colombia. To stay on the cutting edge of cell ministry, it's essential to understand ICM and the "Groups of 12 Model."

GROWTH OF THE
INTERNATIONAL CHARISMATIC MISSION

Pastor César Castellanos instills in his people a vision not only to belong to a cell group, but also to lead one. He believes and teaches that the anointing to lead a cell group rests upon every person in the church, not just a chosen few.

In 1983, Pastor Castellanos was ready to give up after struggling as a pastor for nine years. Then the Lord showed him that the number of converts he would pastor would be more than the stars of the sky and the sand by the seashore. Within months his new church, the Misión Carismática Internacional, had grown to over 200 people.

Charisma magazine reports, "The Castellanos attribute the church's growth to their emphasis on home cell-groups—a focus they believe the Lord gave them after they visited David Yonggi Cho's Yoido Full Gospel Church in South Korea in 1986."[1]

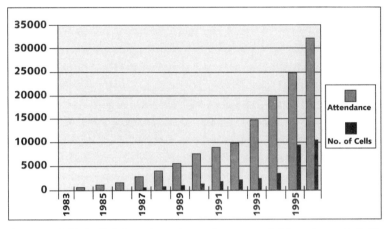

Figure 2 ICM. Celebration Attendance and Number of Cells

GROUPS OF 12 MODEL

After using a cell strategy for seven years Pastor Castellanos received a vision from God that the cell system should be based on the example of Jesus and His 12 disciples. So Pastor Castellanos hand-picked 12 pastors, with whom he continues to meet weekly. (These 12 senior pastors now oversee the satellite churches, the various departments, leadership training, and administrative functions.[2]) Each of these 12 pastors has 12 under him or her, and the process continues down to include each member of the church. Each person remains with the original Group of 12 in which he or she began the discipleship process, unless unusual circumstances necessitate changing to a different group.

In this model, the new cell planter (disciple) meets with his cell leader (discipler) on a continual basis. Until a person finds his or her 12 disciples, that person continues to lead a cell group. After finding 12 disciples (who must be active cell leaders), the discipler primarily concentrates on supervising the 12, although he or she might continue to lead a normal cell group.[3]

It's important to remember that these are not static, ingrown disciples. To be called a "disciple," one must lead a cell group. The Groups of 12 concept is really a way to multiply leadership, and therefore groups, more rapidly. Instead of waiting for an entire cell group to naturally give birth, this concept compels cell leaders to actively look for lay people to lead new cell groups, and thus become disciples in the process.

At ICM, every cell member is a potential cell leader, and this philosophy is followed in practice. As soon as a person is converted, he or she begins a "training track" that leads to cell leadership. Becoming a cell leader is the mark that a person is developing spiritually. In most churches, many are trained in the hope that a few will become leaders. ICM expects it of everyone.

Every cell member is a potential leader of cell leaders. Cell leaders who raise up another leader immediately become overseers. This system does not require a lot of top-level organization and seems to work well on a grass-roots level.

ICM has taken cell groups beyond most cell-based churches, and the results have been staggering. At the beginning of 1997, this is how it looked:

Cells Among Young People[4]	**3,600 cell groups**
Homogeneous Cells In Mother Church	**4,317 cell groups**
Cells in Satellite Churches	**2,683 cell groups**
Total Cell Groups	**13,000 cell groups**

Table 5 ICM: Cell Group Statistical Breakdown

Successful cell leaders at ICM plant a number of new groups, raise up new leaders for other groups, and are now leaders of leaders. If one has accomplished this and is training leaders, that person receives a promotion in the church. Most likely, he or she will be asked to come on the pastoral staff. If that does not happen right away, that person at least will receive clear, positive recognition from within the church.

God clearly is at work at ICM, but it's hard to place this new work in a box. Paul Pierson, professor of mission history at Fuller Seminary, once said, "When God is truly at work, it is often very messy."[5]

The Spirit of God shows the leadership at ICM what to do on a daily basis. Youth Pastor César Fajardo once said that he doesn't want to write a manual about the cell philosophy at ICM because it would be out of date in a few months. He and the other leaders at ICM are radically committed to following the Spirit's leading, even though it means breaking with the established molds of cell-church traditions.

FOUNDATIONAL PRINCIPLES	TRADITIONAL CELL MODEL	ICM
CELL LEADER CARE	Cell leader care is provided by district pastors, zone pastors and supervisors.	Cell leader care is provided by leaders of 12, from the lowest levels to the 12 disciples of Pastor Castellanos.
DIVISION	Cell groups are divided into geographical areas under district pastors, zone leaders and section leaders.	Cell groups are divided by ministerial departments under which each leader has his or her 12 disciples.
JETHRO SYSTEM	Top leadership is raised up to pastor cell leaders under them. There are normally cell leaders, section leaders, zone pastors, and district pastors.	Every leader has 12 under his or her care—from the senior pastor to individual cell leaders. The leader meets weekly with his or her 12.
EVANGELISM	Evangelism is mostly a group activity.	Evangelism is more individual as each leader seeks to gather his or her own group.
LEADERSHIP TRAINING	Potential leaders are trained within the cell and through seminars before beginning cell leadership.	Potential leaders are trained in ongoing classes that take place within the various ministerial departments.
CENTRAL PLANNING	Cell group planning takes place on a centralized level in district offices.	Cell group planning is primarily handled through the different departments.

Table 6 ICM: Distinctions of the Cell Structure

A few other elements stand out at ICM:

CELLS WITHIN THE DEPARTMENTS

Cell groups are organized almost completely under homogenous ministerial departments at ICM.[6] Depending on the size and specificity of the ministry, there might be many cell groups or very few.[7] The larger ministries meet as separate congregations during the week.[8] The major departments have an evangelistic emphasis in their congregational meeting, and altar calls are given.[9] The cell leaders in each of these ministries receive the newcomers, counsel them, call them within 48 hours, and make sure that they are involved in a cell group. Each department has plenty of ministry openings, and the natural link between cell group and ministry helps the newcomer become involved in the church. One important distinction is that the cell group always meets in the home, whereas the large department meeting always takes place in the church.

Relationships are well-maintained in this model, because there is constant contact between leader and disciple. That's part of the reason why Bethany World Prayer Center adopted this model. In the previous leadership pattern, the new leader of the daughter cell often broke relationship with the leader of the mother cell after multiplication. The new leader developed fresh relationships with the supervisor, zone pastor, and district pastor. At ICM and in Bethany's new system, relationships are maintained.

CELL ADMINISTRATION

ICM's organization around the Groups of 12 is a new, creative version of the Jethro concept (Exodus 18). Even higher-level leaders who oversee thousands are still responsible for their Groups of 12.

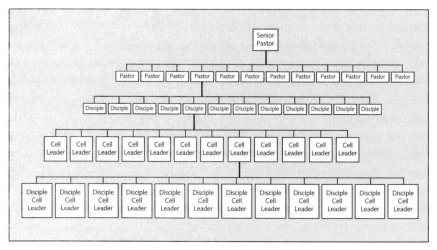

FIGURE 3 ICM: Cell Administrative Structure

In this model, the titles "district pastor," "zone pastor" and "supervisor" are not used. The principle of pastoral care, however, is very evident.

DECENTRALIZATION OF MINISTRY

ICM has more fully decentralized its cell structure than some other cell churches, and this might be a key to its amazing growth. In the traditional cell model, new cell leadership is "passed on" up the hierarchical leadership structure. Others take responsibility for the success of the new cell (e.g. supervisors, zone pastors, district pastors). But in the Groups of 12 Model, the leader of the mother cell has the primary responsibility of developing and pastoring new leadership. The model creates an entrepreneurial challenge for cell leaders to find and develop as many new leaders as possible.

CONTINUOUS MINISTRY

Church never stops at ICM. Services in the main sanctuary run from the early morning prayer meeting until late into the evening. There is rarely a moment when one of the pastors or lay people is not preaching the Word of God, worshipping, or praying.

Prayer continues from 5 to 9 a.m. every day. A different pastor or leader is in charge of each of the four hourly sessions, which draw between 500 and 1,000 people every morning. The church has an all-night prayer meeting every Friday. On special occasions, as drug trafficking and guerrilla warfare worsen, the church dedicates a 24-hour, non-stop period to pray for the country.

ICM members appropriately describe their worship as "explosive." I wrote the following after attending a Saturday night worship service,

> *Here is the future of Colombia—young people touched by the gospel. Here is life! This is Your sovereign work! The young people dance in unison, in a single line using the same hand and feet motions. Two girls lead the entire congregation by modeling the motions. This is a clean, dynamic expression of God's love. The shouts of joy spread like wildfire across the auditorium. This is not just wild, charismatic individualism. There is order everywhere. Each jerk and hand motion is in unity. This is Colombian style. Only Latin Americans could express themselves so well with so little hesitation.*

An entire department is dedicated to this ministry. A full band, complete with precision dancing, livens the sanctuary.

YOUNG PEOPLE

The young people's department, headed by Pastor César Fajardo, is ICM's most successful ministry. In 1997, youth cell groups numbered almost 4,000. In keeping with the model, Pastor Fajardo oversees his 12 disciples; each of those disciples has 12 more, and the process continues down to the new young people who enter each week. Key to the growth is that each disciple also leads a cell group.

About 8,500 young people attended the Saturday night youth service I visited in 1997. At that service, about 500 young people went forward to receive Christ. Each new convert's name is documented and then delivered to a cell group for follow-up. (Each month, the follow-up cards are given to a different one of Pastor Fajardo's 12 disciples, and this ensures that follow-up is evenly distributed.) Another crowning event among the youth is the spiritual retreat *Encuentro* (Encounter), which lasts an entire weekend and serves to draw people to salvation and sanctification.[10] The vision of the young people is contagious, and their goal is to reach 100,000 young people by the year 2000.

BETHANY WORLD PRAYER CENTER

Many believe that Bethany World Prayer Center is the most successful "Pure Cell Model" church in the United States. The reason for Bethany's success: This church learns from others. It has gleaned cell principles from churches all over the world. More recently, it has adopted much of the methodology of the Groups of 12 model and is emphasizing cell planting, especially homogenous groups. About 1,500 pastors attended its biannual cell seminar in November 1997.

CHURCH GROWTH

The cell ministry officially began on April 1993 with 52 groups (made up from prayer ministry). By June 1996, 70 percent of Bethany's adults were attending one of its 312 cell groups. During that time, about 1,500 families joined the church through the cell ministry. Every week, between 25 and 30 people received Christ in the cell groups.[11] Bethany's attendance more than doubled to nearly 8,000 since initiating the cell ministry in 1993.

The initial 52 groups multiplied in three months. Six months later, those group multiplied. In 1996, cells took about a year to multiply. Bethany officially implemented the Groups of 12 Model in early 1997, and cell groups skyrocketed from 320 to 520 groups in a matter of months.

CELL PRINCIPLES FROM BETHANY

Bethany has adapted its cell ministry to the Groups of 12 while retaining the bedrock cell principles gathered from the worldwide cell church movement. Here are a few key principles that can be learned from Bethany's history:

1. The leadership studied other cell models around the world before initiating their own model. Several of these experts—Ralph Neighbour Jr., David Cho, César Castellanos, Karen Hurston—were invited to the church to teach about cell ministry.
2. Extensive cell leadership training took place before initiating the cell ministry.
3. The church was committed to the Pure Cell system from the beginning.
4. The system was fine-tuned as needs were discovered.
5. Prayer was an important factor in the cell system.
6. Goals were established for cell growth.

THE GROUPS OF 12 MODEL

One of the essential principles that Bethany adopted from Colombia is that every person has the anointing for multiplication and the ability to win a multitude. As at ICM, each leader at Bethany seeks out 12 disciples. They scan the congregation to discover potential disciples to add to their group. It's acceptable to have a mixture of mature leaders and potential leaders. Discipling these leaders involves bringing them through basic doctrinal teaching to the point of leading a group. The district pastors, zone pastors and section leaders also have a goal of leading 12 people to the Lord each year.

Zone pastor Bill Satterwhite, for example, converted his six section leaders into disciples. But then he sought out others to add to his group, specifically people with leadership potential who were not in groups. In fact, one of his disciples was a past cell leader who had dropped out.

THE GROUPS OF 12 CONCEPT AT THE CELL LEVEL

Each cell member is encouraged to plant a cell, but the new leader then remains with the original cell for fellowship and discipleship under that cell leader. The idea is to maintain relationships. While the new leader is being discipled, he finds and develops new people. The goal is for every cell member to find five or six non-Christians and start a group with them. This structure allows a person to fulfill God's calling to reap the harvest.

EMPHASIS ON MULTIPLICATION

The pastors at Bethany make it very clear to the cell leaders: "Don't allow your people to think that they are going to stay together forever." Rather, they teach that cell multiplication is the norm and that God places in everything the ability to reproduce itself. Cells are living organisms that have the capacity to reproduce, and district pastors teach that this is the true foundation of the cells.

At least three types of cell multiplication are promoted at Bethany:

1. Internal multiplication. A cell member brings in four or five people and eventually takes them to form a new group.
2. External multiplication. Someone in the cell starts a homogeneous group within the community. This is the main reason for Bethany's current proliferation of cells.
3. Traditional multiplication. This is the mother-daughter method that Bethany has always practiced, only the cell intern takes more responsibility now by developing a team to start a new group. The intern disciples and actively builds relationships with new converts with the goal of starting a new group. Once the intern is discipling five or six people, the new group begins.

HOMOGENOUS CELL GROUPS

Of the over 200 new groups recently started at Bethany World Prayer Center, about 90 percent are homogeneous groups based on relationships already established through work, school or sports. Bethany realizes that most people in the U.S. now find meaningful relationships at the workplace rather than in the neighborhood, and that people are more likely to get involved with those they already know through their current involvements on the job or at school. Thus, homogenous groups are an effective way to evangelize and disciple non-Christians.

The groups' basic goals are building relationships with God and with one another, and reaching the lost. These groups are flexible and can fit into any time-frame. If the members have only 30 minutes for lunch, that's OK; they don't have to finish the whole lesson.

A homogenous leader has a dual commitment to lead his own cell group and to receive discipleship in his original cell group. To avoid schedule conflicts, Bethany asks leaders to limit the new groups to times when they are already meeting with potential members.

This new emphasis at Bethany follows Ralph Neighbour Jr.'s emphasis on interest groups, which he calls "share groups" and "target groups." He says,

There must be a way to go to areas where you do not know anyone—where no natural oikos contacts exist. This is done through "targeting" special groups of people who have a common need or interest. Thus, you and your team may decide there are families living in a certain estate who need a Christian witness. By discovering their needs, interests, etc., you can find a reason to invite these strangers to a 10-week group meeting.[12]

He goes on to say,

Target Groups collect people with common interests. For example, those interested in guitar playing, bicycling, hiking, tennis, swapping computer talk, etc. are areas that readily attract people to meet together. Such interests give you a natural contact with people who do not know you, and who also do not know the Lord. They also collect people with common concerns. Lonely people, parents of rebellious children, diabetics, single parents, victims of substance abuse, widows, the unemployed, etc. are all groups of people who can be reached through Target Groups.[13]

Neighbour recommends that these groups be limited in scope and in duration (10 weeks) to accomplish a particular purpose. But Bethany's homogeneous groups are ongoing and become the cell group for those who attend.

TRAINING NEW CELL LEADERS

Bethany creatively combines personal cell-group training with classroom instruction. Training hasn't changed much since adapting the Groups of 12 model, except that the sessions are offered more frequently. Each district trains new leaders monthly in a five-hour course that combines traditional cell instruction with Bethany's adaptations. To be a leader (as of July 1997), one has to: attend the church for six months; be an active member of a Touch Group; take a Leadership Discipleship Track (six-weeks training in cell group, four-weeks training in classroom); and attend one of the five-hour intern training seminars that are offered monthly in each district. The 48-week process that takes a new believer all the way to leadership is called "Accomplishing the Four Purposes." As part of ongoing training, Pastor Larry addresses all leaders at a monthly leadership summit, where he presents the vision for the month and the month's cell lessons.

CELL ORGANIZATION

Bethany's organizational structure is impressive. The cell offices contain a mailbox for each cell leader, tracking charts on the wall, and statistical accountability for every level of leadership. Strategizing and administration still takes place in the district offices. The leadership structure of district pastor, zone pastor, and section leader is also the same. Statistical reports are still required of every cell leader.[14]

FOLLOW-UP

Zone pastors still greet new converts after the celebration service. The baby Christians are assigned to a cell group, and the cell and section leaders make an immediate visit. After joining a Touch group, the new convert is invited to a "first step" weekend retreat at the church, following the pattern at ICM. After the retreat, the disciple follows the normal training class with the goal of eventually becoming a cell leader.

SENIOR PASTOR INVOLVEMENT

The role of the senior pastor is crucial to the long-term success of the cell ministry. Bethany's Pastor Larry Stockstill models his commitment to cell ministry by his personal involvement. He addresses cell seminars held at Bethany each year. Each week, Pastor Larry:

1. Prepares the cell lesson.
2. Makes a surprise visit to a cell group to find out whether his ideas work (e.g., cell lesson, etc.).
3. Links his Sunday morning message to the cell ministry.
4. Encourages with fresh vision all of the cell leaders.[15]
5. Presents the new daughter cells before the congregation for prayer and encouragement.
6. Maintains the cell focus and guards against programs sapping the cell vision.
7. Meets with his cell staff.
8. Meets with twelve teenage boys that he is equipping as leaders.

MISSION VISION

Bethany is committed to planting cell churches all over the world, and this commitment reaches deep into the purse strings of the church. Bethany's missions budget was $600,000 in 1985, and it has increased $100,000 every year since. In 1996 the church gave $1.8 million to missions.[16]

Bethany requires its homegrown missionaries to first serve successfully as cell leaders. Pastor Larry's ideal is for every missionary candidate first to multiply a cell group and also serve in an upper-level cell leadership position (i.e., section leader, zone leader, district pastor).[17] Bethany currently supports more than 90 of its own missionaries who serve in more than 24 countries around the world.[18]

THE CHRISTIAN CENTER OF GUAYAQUIL

CCG is an exciting model in Guayaquil, Ecuador, that is multiplying cell groups rapidly. From 1992 to 1996, CCG grew from 16 cells to 1,600—averaging 396 new groups per year. According to the cell manual, the small groups at CCG are expected to give birth within six months, and this is the goal of every cell leader. Multiplication does occur, but CCG also plants many cells from scratch. Although exact figures are not available, one leader estimates that 80 percent of new cells are planted vs. 20 percent that are birthed through multiplication. CCG does not have a strict timeline for closing a group if it does not multiply.

The machinery in place at CCG to start and pastor new cell groups is impressive. This church is committed to reach Guayaquil (over 2 million people) through cell groups and to gather in the great harvest there.

EVANGELISM THROUGH THE CELL GROUP

Before starting cells, CCG administered a complete Evangelism Explosion (E.E.) program. Although CCG still hosts an E.E. clinic each year, the church adapts E.E. to its cell ministry. Cell leaders are encouraged to take E.E., and E.E. visits are delegated according to zones in each district. More decisions are made for Christ in the cell groups than in the church services, and those who do receive Christ in the services usually are prepared beforehand by the cell groups.

It is important to note that leading a person to baptism, and not just to accepting Christ, is the goal of cell leaders. No one in the church is baptized unless he or she is part of a cell group. Baptismal applications are brought to the church by the cell leader, not by the applicant.

Once a person is baptized, attending a cell group, and expresses interest in leadership, he or she attends a four-week training class that covers the main points of the CCG manual on cell group ministry. A person officially can lead a cell group after completing the four-week course, although further training is encouraged. CCG offers various levels of leadership and biblical training, from this initial four-week class to a full Bible degree from CCG's Bible College.

LEADING TWO CELL GROUPS

So many new groups are able to start at CCG because, on average, every leader directs two groups. If someone is willing to open his or her home for a cell group, the zone pastor frequently will ask one of the existing cell leaders to direct the new group.

GOAL SETTING

Each zone leader sets specific goals concerning the number of new cells, cell attendance, conversions and baptisms. New goals are drawn up each year in conjunction with district pastors and are submitted to Pastor Jerry Smith for final approval. Each week, district pastors evaluate their zone pastor's progress; the zone pastor evaluates the superintendents; and the superintendents encourage the cell leaders based on goals. A statistical analysis is made every trimester (based on percentages) to show leaders how close they are to reaching their goals.

VISITATION

Each zone pastor makes approximately 40 visits each week to cell members, new converts and visitors for a total of about 920 visits a week. These zone pastors are always alert to the possibility of opening a new home for a cell plant, multiplying an existing cell group, or recognizing emerging leaders. Many new groups start as a result of the diligent visits by zone pastors.

Elevation in ministry at CCG is largely based on successfully starting and leading cell groups. Most zone and district pastors earn their position because of past success. Thus, the hope of many superintendents and cell leaders is to one day become a zone pastor or district pastor.

FAITH COMMUNITY BAPTIST CHURCH

FCBC's leadership realizes that its normal process of mother-daughter cell multiplication is not producing the desired result even though the plans and programs for cell evangelism are excellent. Net cell gain has stagnated in the last several years, but FCBC hopes to turn this around by emphasizing cell planting. Small groups formed through cell planting offers a ray of hope to FCBC.

THE VISION FOR CELL PLANTING

District Pastor Leong Wing Keen says that the 1998 annual cell conference will emphasize cell planting. The Rev. Richard Ong, executive director of Touch Ministries International, says that the Holy Spirit is waking up the worldwide cell church with similar ideas, specifically mentioning Ralph Neighbour Jr. and the cell planting success at ICM in Colombia. Ong explains that endless mother-daughter cell multiplication is just not possible because a person's *oikos* relationships eventually run dry. Campus/Combat Ministry Director Chua Seng Lee explains that cell planting at FCBC originated in his district with university students, and that this idea is taking hold throughout the church.

HOW CELLS ARE PLANTED

As of April 1997, the cell-planting concept mainly was still in the idea stage at FCBC. Two cell-planting techniques are being utilized, however. In the first, a cell chooses a target and begins prayer walking the area. The cell then establishes contact with someone in the targeted area (either a non-Christian or a church sympathizer) who is willing to open his or her home for a cell. Several stronger members (spiritual fathers) from the mother group meet with the new group while continuing to attend the mother cell. The goal is to eventually form two separate cells.

The second method links cell planting with FCBC's three major harvest events. The homes of those who receive Christ at these events are targeted for cell plants. These new converts often are culturally or geographically distant from the mother group and so are not naturally assimilated into it. Again, a few of the mother cell's stronger members form new cells comprised of these new believers. The stronger members continue attending their own cell, while seeking to establish a new group.

12

UNDERSTAND MOTHER-DAUGHTER MULTIPLICATION

I n this traditional cell church multiplication method, an existing cell group oversees the creation of a daughter group by providing people, leadership and personal care. Several cell churches around the world have perfected this method and are ready to teach the rest of us what they've learned.

ELIM CHURCH

EC in San Salvador, led by Pastor Mario Vega, is a premier example of expansion through mother-daughter cell multiplication. Elim has grown to 5,400 strong cell groups in just 10 years. Approximately 120,000 people attend cell groups each week, averaging 21 people per cell. Elim's key appears to be a combination of clear goal-setting, team planning, and excellent leadership follow-up (through statistical control and the Jethro system).

When EC adopted the cell system in 1985, the mother church Elim immediately closed 25 affiliated churches in San Salvador and unified them into one city church. Many cell groups then were started from scratch. While the initial goal was to open as many groups as possible without much regard for quality or multiplication, the system now assures quality control while maintaining the vision for rapid multiplication.

Elim aims to penetrate the entire city of San Salvador with the gospel, primary through mother-daughter cell multiplication. (Some cell planting is occurring in newly targeted areas.[1]) Pastor

Vega says that of the 5,400 cell groups, about 1,000 were cell plants; the other 4,400 resulted from mother-daughter cell group multiplication.

At least three aspects of Elim's system are worth noting:

1. EC does not close cells that fail to multiply. Everything possible is done to keep groups alive.
2. EC will not multiply a cell until 20 adults are attending the group meetings. This rule is strictly enforced, unless the host home is too small for a group that size or the new daughter team is at a high state of readiness.
3. EC multiplies the nucleus before multiplying the cell. Expansion of the leadership team is one of the major goals of the church-wide Thursday night planning meetings. Great care is given to prepare the new nucleus that will guide the daughter cell group.

REASONS FOR SUCCESS

Throughout Latin America EC is known for multiplying strong cell groups. There are at least four reasons for this success:

1. **Goal Setting**. Each zone sets a "simple" goal for each year: double the number of groups, attendance, conversions and baptisms. These goals are then divided by four to arrive at a quarterly goal. All cell leadership at every level is placed on a list according to how close they come to reaching their goals. Each category of goal (baptism, attendance, etc.) is given a certain weight. All leaders are compared to one another according to how well they're working toward 100 percent growth. The "healthy competition" among pastors regarding those goals fuels the high degree of motivation to grow.
2. **Team Planning**. The Thursday night team planning meeting seems to be essential to cell group growth and the eventual multiplication. At these meetings, strategies to reach new people are developed, visitation is planned, and multiplication is envisioned. The new team begins to take shape during these planning sessions.

3. **Organization**. Elim has developed a highly efficient system of statistical tracking that counts each of the 120,000 people who attend the cell groups during the week. The system is indigenous.[2] The statistical follow-up of every meeting gives pastors and supervisors a progress report of each cell, and it motivates the leaders to reach out. In addition, the smooth functioning Jethro system provides help and training for cell leaders. These two aspects of the cell system work together to maintain a growth rhythm.

4. **Evangelism**. The most effective form of cell outreach at EC is friendship evangelism. Leaders instruct their groups to make friends, win their confidence, and then invite them to the meeting. The goal is for each of these people to receive Christ and become a member of the church. Other evangelism is practiced (door-to-door visitation, movies, dinners, etc.), but the most effective form takes place among family, neighbors and friends.

LEADERSHIP TRAINING

Each district offers ongoing, four-week training courses for potential leaders. As one group graduates, the next begins. These classes, designed to instill Elim's cell philosophy, usually are taught by a two-person team (two zone pastors or the district pastor and zone pastor.

FIRST WEEK	• The Calling to Lead • The Vision of the Cell Group • The Reason for Cell Groups
SECOND WEEK	• Requirements and Characteristics of Leadership • Lesson Preparation
THIRD WEEK	• How the Cell Groups Operate • How the Cell Groups Multiply
FOURTH WEEK	• Organization and Control • Final Exam

Table 7. Training Course at Elim

LOVE ALIVE CHURCH

Love Alive Church in Tegucigalpa, Honduras, approaches cell-group multiplication with an incredibly effective creativity. In September 1996, the church opened 200 new groups simultaneously. Several aspects of cell-multiplication methodology are unique to this church.

SIMULTANEOUS MULTIPLICATION

Cell groups at LAC multiply at the same time and normally on a pre-determined date each year. Only about 10 percent of new groups open at other times. LAC aims for the one-year mark because leadership believes cells take that long to solidify.[3] Focusing on an overall multiplication date results in several advantages:

1. Top leadership can plan more concretely concerning future goals.
2. The training of new leadership teams can take place at the same time in the church.
3. Leaders of sectors, zones, and districts can consolidate their time and energy by focusing on one particular time period of multiplication.
4. New cell groups opening together receive tremendous support, ensuring that weaker groups won't fall through the cracks.
5. The church can better focus its prayer and support.

10-MEMBER CELLS

LAC used to multiply a group at 15 people, but maintaining 15 people over a long period proved difficult. A few years ago, leadership decided that a cell would be a prime candidate to multiply if it averaged 10 members. If a cell is regularly attended by seven to nine people, the supervisor often asks the leader to make specific evangelistic goals to reach new people. It is possible, however, to multiply a group with only eight people, because the key is having a strong new leadership team in place. If a cell group does not grow, however, steps are taken to discover the spiritual condition of the cell leadership team.

TEAM CONCEPT

Each new cell must have a three-person leadership nucleus (leader, assistant leader and treasurer) before a cell is birthed. Every month, the supervisor reports to the zone leader about the condition of the groups, including the formation of new leadership teams, under his or her care. The zone pastor accordingly counsels and encourages the supervisor concerning the preparation of the new leadership team that will, in effect, serve as missionaries. The information is passed on to the district pastor, who ensures through the zone pastors and supervisors that the leadership teams are ready to operate.

RELATIONSHIP WITH MOTHER CELL

Dixie Rosales, LAC's director of cell ministry, attributes the high quality of cell groups to the mother-daughter relationship. He believes that the established cell must take responsibility for the health of the new group if the new group is going to succeed.[4]

LAC cells meet on Wednesday night. When a massive multiplication occurs, the new cells meet on Tuesday night for the first three months. For these three months, the mother cell's leadership team directs the Wednesday cell and also attends the new Tuesday cell group to offer support and encouragement.[5] After the first three months, the new groups begin to meet on Wednesday night and become official cell groups.

COUNSELING AND ASSESSMENT FOR TWO MONTHS

Counseling and assessment takes place for the first two months after a massive multiplication. Every other Thursday night, the new cell team (leader, assistant and treasurer) meets with the immediate supervisor to receive edification from Scripture, prayer, and counseling.[6] Along with the section supervisor, the district pastor and the zone pastor must also attend these assessment meetings.

THE MULTIPLICATION PROCESS AT LAC

The process for starting new groups is taken so seriously at LAC that it begins five months before the multiplication date. Cell leaders work hard to develop new leadership from within their groups. These potential leaders are baptized, take discipleship classes, and participate in the life of the cell group. The seven-stop process is outlined below:

1. **Goals for multiplication**. The process begins when a cell leader communicates the goal for multiplication to the area supervisor, who reports this to the zone pastor, who in turn tells the district pastor. The district pastor meets with the director of cell ministry to assess the number of groups that can multiply. Final approval of how many new cells will open rests with the head pastor.

2. **Host home and new leadership team**. The cell leader and team searches for a home in the same area that will provide an acceptable environment for a new cell. The supervisor meets with each leadership team monthly, and one of the objectives is to discover, stimulate, and prepare the cell team to give birth to a new group.

3. **Selecting the leadership team**. Because a new group cannot start without a leadership team (leader, assistant leader and treasurer[7]), every cell strives to form this new leadership nucleus—LAC calls them "missionaries"—that will open a new growth group.

4. **Interviews**. In the third month of multiplication preparation, the district pastor interviews new leaders about their devotional life, marriage, available time for the church, and personal attitudes. This interview is to ensure that the leader is able to remain strong under pressure and that the cell group has a good chance of surviving.[8]

5. **Training and presentation**. During the fourth month, the new leadership teams attend a special training session that covers such topics as: how to lead the lesson, how to evangelize, how to develop worship, and how to confront problems in the group.[9] Before multiplication, the new leadership teams are presented before the church, and the whole church prays and fasts for the success of the new groups.

6. **Cell group evangelism**. In the fifth and final month, there is an intense effort to evangelize in the area in which the new growth group will open. The new leadership team, members from the mother group, and even the area supervisor evangelize the neighborhood together.[10] Finally, the day comes for the groups to open.

7. **Assessment**. As previously explained, the new cell teams meet with their new supervisors and zone pastors for prayer, encouragement, and counseling. This is an essential time for the leadership to receive vision and help.

ELEVATION IN MINISTRY

Moving up the cell ministry leadership ladder depends on several factors, including the person's time commitment, spiritual commitment, or God's calling on their life. Personal success clearly leads to greater responsibility at LAC.[11] Those in top leadership positions have experienced success in multiplication and leadership. Amazingly, all district and zone pastors hold full-time jobs and are not paid by the church, although they have incredible authority within the church.

Some aspects of the cell meeting are distinct at Love Alive:

1. Everyone in the meeting receives a copy of the lesson.
2. The order of the meeting is flexible.
3. Anyone of the team members can lead the lesson.
4. The meeting house does not change week after week.

DOVE CHRISTIAN FELLOWSHIP

Pastor Larry Kreider never intended to start a church. He tried to integrate the van loads of young people whom he had won to Christ into the existing church structures. Yet, for some reason, the new wine kept bursting the old, existing wineskins. He finally yielded to God's call on his life and started DOVE Christian Fellowship in 1980. From humble beginnings, the church grew to over 2,000 people in 10 years. Pastor Larry's congregation spread out across a seven-county area of Pennsylvania. He describes his experiment this way,

> *These believers met in more than 100 cell groups during the week and on Sunday mornings met in clusters of cells (congregations) in five different locations. . . . Our goal was to multiply the cells and celebrations, beginning new Sunday morning celebrations and new cell groups in other areas as God gave the increase. . . . During these years, churches were planted in Scotland, Brazil, and Kenya. These overseas churches were built on Jesus Christ and on these same underground house-to-house principles.*[12]

Pastor Larry believes that multiplication and reproduction most clearly demonstrate God's heartbeat for a lost and dying world. He says that if we are going to be in tune with God, we must be willing and committed to rapid multiplication.[13] In May 1996, DOVE Christian Fellowship had 5,000 believers worshipping in five distinct congregations. The cell groups are the heart and base of the church. Larry describes his commitment to the pure cell paradigm of ministry in his 1995 book entitled *House to House*.

FAITH COMMUNITY BAPTIST CHURCH

Since FCBC initiated the cell structure in May 1988, mother-daughter multiplication has been the norm. The leadership expects each cell to multiply within one year; if it fails to do so, the group is integrated into other existing ones. FCBC's creative organizational system combines the efficiency of the geographical district with the need for specialized ministry better than any other cell church. Cell multiplication occurs within each district.

GEOGRAPHICAL DISTRICTS

These districts are described as homogeneous with heterogeneous cell groups. The districts reach out to families who are culturally similar. Groups with children are called intergenerational cells. District divisions encourage cells to reach out to neighbors, as well as to assimilate church converts who live nearby. The goal for the year 2000 is 5,000 cell groups in Singapore.[14]

YOUTH ZONE

This zone reaches youth ages 12 to 19 and requires more supervision than others. Instead of the normal ratio of one zone supervisor to five cells, youth zone supervisors oversee only three cells. Youth cells evangelize through personal, relational evangelism instead of evangelistic events.

CAMPUS AND COMBAT DISTRICT

This district serves young adults ages 18 to 25. Chua Seng Lee, Campus and Combat director, establishes cells on university campuses and in military camps in Singapore. In this district, the standard FCBC cell lessons are adapted, leadership commitment is often shorter, and more cells are planted. Youth Zone graduates enter this district after high school; young people older than 25 graduate into the district cells. Only future workers are allowed to stay within this district after age 25.

MUSIC ZONE

This creative zone is comprised mainly of members from Touch Music Ministry. Cells are fully integrated with people not involved in music, though members often are friends of those in music ministry. Because of the music ministry's high demands, leadership integrated the cell and the ministry. Jim Egli wrote in 1993, "The reason why they are organized into a separate Zone is so that those in the music ministry do not need to develop two sets of relationships. Since the music ministry involves considerable time commitment, this eases their time and is freeing to them."[15]

CHINESE DISTRICT

Although English unifies the four major languages spoken in Singapore, not everyone can speak English well. This district reaches out to non-English speakers through cells. One Sunday morning service also is dedicated to them.

HANDICAP DISTRICT

This district reaches the hearing-impaired, wheelchair-bound, intellectually disabled, and visually handicapped people. These people often do not feel wanted nor cared for in normal geographical cell groups, but their needs are met in this district. This district office is organized with the same charts and procedures as the other districts.

The homogeneous nature of each district helps multiplication to occur more naturally. The creative organizational structure at FCBC is a model to the cell church worldwide. Cell multiplication flows more rapidly along homogeneous lines and FCBC has structured itself to reap the harvest.

13

A PARABLE

A man once had a beautiful garden which yielded rich and abundant food. His neighbor saw it and planted his own garden the next spring. But he did nothing to it. There was no watering, no cultivating or fertilizing. In the fall, he returned to his devastated garden. There was no fruit and it was overgrown with weeds. He concluded that gardening did not work. On further thought he pondered that the problem was bad soil or maybe he lacked a "green thumb" like his neighbor.

Meanwhile, a third neighbor began gardening. His garden did not immediately yield as much as the first man but he worked hard and continued learning new skills. As he toiled, he learned. As he put his new learning into practice year after year, his garden reaped an increasingly abundant harvest.

I hope the truth of this parable is obvious. I traversed the globe to discover the secrets of small group growth. Interestingly, it was the same principles in every country, culture and church that made the difference between cell growth or stagnation. Hard work and the steady application of proven principles set apart the successful group leaders. The insights outlined in this book will work for you if you are willing to pay the price. They are not magical principles. They require time and effort.

My research revealed that successful cell leaders spent more time seeking God's face, dependent on Him for the direction of their cell group. They prepared themselves first and afterwards they prepared the lesson. They prayed diligently for their members as well as non-Christian contacts. Their goals for multiplication were revealed in the listening room and these leaders simply obeyed marching orders.

But successful cell leaders did not stop with prayer. They came down from the mountain top to interact with real people, full of problems and pain. They pastored their cell members, visiting them regularly. Those who multiplied their groups were not immune to "dark nights of the soul." They also passed through the valleys but they declined to stay there. They refused to allow the obstacles—that all cell leaders face—to overcome them. They fastened their eyes on one goal—reaching a lost world for Christ through cell multiplication.

You too can lead your cell group to growth and multiplication. This "anointing" doesn't rest on a chosen few. The introverted, the uneducated, and those in the lower social bracket were just as successful as their counterparts. Nor did one particular gift of the Spirit distinguish those who could multiply their groups from those who could not. Successful cell leaders don't depend on their own gifts. They rely on the Holy Spirit as they marshal the entire cell to reach family, friends, and acquaintances.

As I trekked around the world to discover these principles, I met successful cell leaders in all eight different cultures. It became clear to me that culture is not the determining factor in cell multiplication. Whether a cell leader initiates a group in Korea, the United States or Latin America, success depends on hard work and the steady application of these basic principles. I also met cell leaders in each culture who concluded that "gardening didn't work," thus producing very little. Beyond a willingness to work hard, there are two more principles that must grip you.

First, be crystal clear about your goal—cell multiplication. The successful cell churches around the world are focused on growth. They don't waver on this point. Small-group multiplication embraces so many other leadership qualities that it must be the central focus of cell ministry. Most people equate cell multiplication with evangelism, but evangelism is only part of the equation. The leader who has multiplied his or her group has developed and trained new leaders, ignited a passion for evangelism, prayed fervently for each member, pastored the core members, visited the new ones, and communicated a clear vision of cell multiplication to the rest of the group.

Secondly, you must make leadership development your chief priority. Successful small group leaders view each member as a potential leader. In dynamic cell churches (like ICM), everyone is a potential leader and the genetic code of cell multiplication is instilled in each believer from the onset.

The home cell group explosion is rippling around the world, but it hasn't yet reached its peak. The purpose of this book is to help you fine-tune your small group ministry so that it can have a powerful impact in a hurting world. Whether your small group plants new cells or gives birth to daughter cells, the goal is the same—explosive cell growth that leads to multiplication. If you work hard, seek God, and patiently put the principles of cell growth into practice, you will see an abundant harvest!

APPENDIX A

Questionnaire: English
Personal Information

Important: Only choose one box under each question

1. Country identification
   - ❑ Colombia (1)
   - ❑ Ecuador (2)
   - ❑ Peru (3)
   - ❑ Honduras (4)
   - ❑ El Salvador (5)
   - ❑ Korea (6)
   - ❑ Singapore (7)
   - ❑ United States (8)

2. Gender of the leader
   - ❑ Masculine (1)
   - ❑ Feminine (2)

3. Social level
   - ❑ Poor (1)
   - ❑ Middle lower class (2)
   - ❑ Middle class (3)
   - ❑ Middle upper class (4)

4. What is your age? _____

5. What is your civil status?
   - ❑ Married (1)
   - ❑ Single (2)
   - ❑ Divorced (3)
   - ❑ Separated (4)
   - ❑ Living together (5)

6. What is your occupation?
   - ❑ Blue collar (1)
   - ❑ White collar (2)
   - ❑ Professional (3)
   - ❑ Teacher (4)
   - ❑ Other (5)

7. What is your level of education?
   - ❑ Elementary (1)
   - ❑ High School (2)
   - ❑ University (3)
   - ❑ Graduate level (4)
   - ❑ Other (5)

8. How many assistant leaders do you have in your group?
   - ❑ 0 assistant leaders (1)
   - ❑ 1 assistant leaders (2)
   - ❑ 2 assistant leaders (3)
   - ❑ 3 or more assistant leaders (4)

9. How long have you known Jesus Christ?
   - ❑ Six months (1)
   - ❑ One year (2)
   - ❑ Two years (3)
   - ❑ Three years (4)
   - ❑ More than three years (5)

10. How much Bible training have you received?
    - ❑ Less than the average cell member (1)
    - ❑ Same as the average cell member (2)
    - ❑ A little more than the average cell member (3)
    - ❑ Much more than the average cell member (4)

11. How much time do you spend in daily devotions? (e.g., prayer, Bible reading)
    - ❑ 0-.5 hours (1)
    - ❑ .5 hours (2)
    - ❑ 1 hour (3)
    - ❑ 1.5 hours (4)
    - ❑ More than 1.5 hours (5)

12. How much time do you spend praying for the members of your group?
    - ❑ Daily (1)
    - ❑ Every other day (2)
    - ❑ Once a week (3)
    - ❑ Sometimes (4)

13. How much time do you spend each week preparing for your cell group lesson?
    - ❑ 0-1 hours (1)
    - ❑ 1-3 hours (2)
    - ❑ 3-5 hours (3)
    - ❑ 5-7 hours (4)
    - ❑ More (5)

INFORMATION ABOUT CELL GROUP LEADERSHIP

14. As the leader of the cell group, how many times per month do you contact the members of your group?
    - ❑ 1-2 times per month (1)
    - ❑ 3-4 times per month (2)
    - ❑ 5-7 times per month (3)
    - ❑ 8 or more times per month (4)

15. How many times per month does your group meet for social occasions outside of the regular cell group meeting?
    - ❑ 0 (1)
    - ❑ 1 (2)
    - ❑ 2, 3 (3)
    - ❑ 4, 5 (4)
    - ❑ 6 or more (5)

16. As the leader of the cell group, how many times per month do you contact new people?
    - ❑ 1-2 times per month (1)
    - ❑ 3-4 times per month (2)
    - ❑ 5-7 times per month (3)
    - ❑ 8 or more times per month (4)

17. How many times each month do you encourage the cell members to invite their friends to the cell group?
    - ❑ Each cell meeting (1)
    - ❑ Every other cell meeting (2)
    - ❑ Sometimes (3)
    - ❑ Not very much (4)

18. In the last month, how many visitors did you have in your cell group?
    - ❑ 0 visitors (1)
    - ❑ 1 visitor (2)
    - ❑ 2-3 visitors (3)
    - ❑ 4-5 visitors (4)
    - ❑ 6 visitors (5)

19. Do you know when your group is going to multiply?
    - ❑ Yes (1)
    - ❑ No (2)
    - ❑ Not sure (3)

20. In your opinion, which of the following areas helps you most in your cell ministry?
    - ❑ Personality (1)
    - ❑ Biblical Training (2)
    - ❑ Spiritual commitment (3)
    - ❑ The gifts of the Holy Spirit (4)
    - ❑ Pastoral care (5)

21. What is your primary spiritual gift?
    - ❑ Gift of evangelism (1)
    - ❑ Gift of leadership (2)
    - ❑ Gift of pastoral care (3)
    - ❑ Gift of mercy (4)
    - ❑ Gift of teaching (5)
    - ❑ Other (6)

22. In your opinion, what is the most important reason why some cell groups are able to multiply?
    - ❑ Effectiveness of leader (1)
    - ❑ Hard work of the group members (2)
    - ❑ The location where the group meets (3)
    - ❑ The material that the group uses (4)
    - ❑ The spirituality of the group (5)

23. With regard to your personality, which of the following is your tendency?
    - ❑ Introverted (1)
    - ❑ Extroverted (2)
    - ❑ Neither (3)

24. With regard to your personality, which of the following is your tendency?
    ❑ Relaxed (1)
    ❑ Anxious (2)
    ❑ Neither (3)

25 How long has your cell group been functioning? (weeks that it has been in existence) _____

26. What is the level of homogeneity in your group? (e.g., similar race, social class)
    ❑ Very high (1)
    ❑ High (2)
    ❑ Medium (3)
    ❑ Low (4)
    ❑ Very low (5)

27. Has your group multiplied yet?
    ❑ Yes (1)
    ❑ No (2)

28. How much time did it take for you to multiply your group? _____

29. How many times has your group multiplied since you've become the leader?
    ❑ 0 times (1)
    ❑ 1 time (2)
    ❑ 2 times (3)
    ❑ 3 times (4)
    ❑ 4 or more times (5)

NOTES

INTRODUCTION
[1] David Yonggi Cho, *Successful Home Cell Groups*. (Miami, FL: Logos International 1981)

CHAPTER 1
[1] Jim Egli, director of new products at TOUCH Outreach Ministries and a Ph.D. student at Regent University, adapted my questionnaire (improved it) and administered it to 200 cell leaders at Bethany World Prayer Center in Baker, La. His findings coincide with mine, and thus confirm the validity of this study.
[2] At YFGC, approximately 153,000 people attend the mother church on any given Sunday. There are, however, an additional 100,000 people attending the ten YFGC satellite churches in different parts of Seoul, Korea. These satellite churches are considered extensions of the mother church and are therefore included in the mother church attendance, thus totaling 253,000 people in the Sunday morning worship services. The 25,000 cell groups only operate in the mother church. It's unknown how many cells function in the ten extension churches (official statistics at YFGC only mention the 25,000 cell groups of the mother church).

CHAPTER 2
[1] Elizabeth Farrell,"Aggressive Evangelism in an Asian Metropolis," *Charisma* magazine, Jan. 1996, pp. 54-56.
[2] Ralph W. Neighbour Jr., *Where Do We Go From Here: A Guidebook for the Cell Group Church* (Houston, TX: Touch Publications, 1990), p. 193.
[3] Robert Wuthnow, *I Come Away Stronger: How Small Groups Are Shaping American Religion* (Grand Rapids, MI: William B. Eerdmans Publishing Company, 1994), p. 370.
[4] Wuthnow, p. 371.
[5] Lyle E. Schaller, *The New Reformation: Tomorrow Arrived Yesterday* (Nashville, TN: Abingdon Press, 1995), p. 14.
[6] Michael C. Mack, *The Synergy Church* (Grand Rapids, MI: Baker Book House), p.53.
[7] Mack, p. 94
[8] Dale Galloway, *The Small Group Book* (Grand Rapids, MI: Fleming H. Revell, 1995), p. 150.
[9] Carl George, *Prepare Your Church for the Future* (Grand Rapids, MI: Baker Book House, 1991), p. 99.
[10] *The American Heritage Dictionary of the English Language, Third Edition* © 1992 by Houghton Mifflin Co.
[11] Ibid.
Excerpted from *Compton's Interactive Encyclopedia.* © 1994, 1995 Compton's NewMedia, Inc.
[12] Mikel Neumann, *Home Groups for Urban Cultures: Biblical Small Group Ministry on Five Continents.* Forthcoming, 1997. Used by permission of the Billy Graham Center, Wheaton College, Wheaton, IL 60187-5593.
[13] Larry Kreider, *House to House* (Houston, TX: Touch Publications), p.84
[14] Neighbour, p. 247.
[15] C. Kirk Hadaway, Stuart A. Wright, and Francis DuBose, *Home Cell Groups and House Churches.* (Nashville, TN: Broadman Press, 1987), p.66

[16] Howard A. Snyder, *The Radical Wesley and Patterns for Church Renewal* (Downers Grove, IL: Inter Varsity Press, 1980), p. 63.

[17] William Brown, "Growing the Church Through Small Groups in the Australian Context." D.Min. dissertation. Fuller Theological Seminary, 1992, p. 39.

[18] Doyle L. Young, *New Life for Your Church*. (Grand Rapids, MI: Baker Book House, 1989), p. 113.

[19] George G. Hunter III, *To Spread the Power: Church Growth in the Wesleyan Spirit* (Nashville, TN: Abingdon Press, 1987), p. 58.

[20] Brown, p. 39.

[21] Hunter, p. 56.

[22] William Walter Dean, in his dissertation on the Wesley class system, writes, "Cell division was much less common than might have been expected. The formation of new classes was by far the most frequent approach to growth." William Walter Dean, "Disciplined Fellowship: The Rise and Decline of Cell Groups in British Methodism." (University of Iowa, Ph.D. dissertation, 1985), 266.

[23] Hunter, p. 57.

[24] T.A. Hegre, "La Vida Que Agrada a Dios." *Mensaje De La Cruz*. April-May: 8-16, 1993, p, 8.

[25] Peggy Kannaday, editor of *Church Growth and the Home Cell System* (Seoul, Korea: Church Growth International, 1995) details Cho's emphasis on cell evangelism (p.41).

[26] Hadaway, p. 17.

[27] The women at Yoido church are fully integrated into the cell system, but a much lower portion of the men participate in the cells. Recent statistics show 19,704 women's cell groups, 3,612 men's cell groups, 569 children's cells (Kannaday 1995:139).

CHAPTER 3

[1] David Yonggi Cho, <u>Recruiting Staff For a Large Church</u>. Church Growth Lectures. Audio tape 2. Fuller Theological Seminar, School of World Mission. Pasadena, CA, 1984.

[2] David Yonggi Cho, <u>Church Growth</u>. Manual No. 7. (Seoul, Korea: Church Growth International, 1995) pp. 13-16.

[3] C. Peter Wagner, <u>Your Spiritual Gifts Can Help Your Church Grow</u> (Glendale, CA: Regal Books, 1994), p. 157.

[4] This quote is from an e-mail that Jim Egli sent to his statistical research professor at Regent University in spring 1997.

CHAPTER 4

[1] Robert J. Clinton, *The Making of a Leader* (Colorado Springs: NavPress, 1988), p. 127.

[2] Clinton, p. 69.

[3] Ralph Neighbour, *The Shepherd's Guidebook: A Leader's Guide for the Cell Group Church* (Houston, TX: Touch Publications, 1992), p. 49.

[4] Neighbour, 1992, p. 48.

[5] Carl George, *How To Break Growth Barriers* (Grand Rapids, MI: Baker Book House, 1993), p. 38.

[6] Oswaldo Cruzado, "El Tiempo Devocional" Un manual de la Alianza en el Distrito Hispano del Este (The Christian and Missionary Alliance, n.d.), p. 1.

[7] As quoted in Peter Wagner, Prayer Shield (Ventura CA: Regal Books, 1992), p. 86.

[8] Wagner, 1992, p. 86.

[9] Charles R. Swindoll, *Intimacy with the Almighty* (Dallas, TX: Word Publishing, 1996), p. 28.

[10] Swindoll, pp. 17-18.

[11] Neighbour, 1992, p. 50.

[12] Matthew Henry, in Matthew Henry's Commentary on the Bible (Peabody, MA: Hendrickson Publishers, 1991) on CD-ROM, writes, "We may be present in spirit with those churches and Christians from whom we are absent in body; for the communion of saints is a spiritual thing. Paul had heard concerning the Colossians that they were orderly and regular; and though he had never seen them, nor was present with them, he tells them he could easily think himself among them, and look with pleasure upon their good behavior."

[13] C. Peter Wagner, *Prayer Shield* (Ventura, CA: Regal Books, 1992).

[14] Brother Lawrence, *The Practice of the Presence of God* (Grand Rapids: MI: Fleming H. Revell) p. 31.

[15] A.W. Tozer, *The Pursuit of God* (Harrisburg, PA: Christian Publications, Inc.), p. 91.

[16] Andrew Murray, *With Christ in the School of Prayer* (New York: Loizeaux Brothers, Inc., Publishers, n.d.), pp. 16-23.

[17] Ed Silvoso, in *That None Should Perish* (Ventura, CA: Regal Books, 1994), talks about an effective strategy of establishing small groups dedicated to praying for the lost (pp. 253-264). Bruno Radi (Nazarene Church) has established a movement of prayer cells in Latin America.

[18] C. Peter Wagner, in *"Churches That Pray"* (Ventura, CA: Regal Books, 1993), explains the prayer movement phenomenon (pp. 13-32). Wagner is at the forefront of this movement as the director of the A.D. 2000 Prayer Track.

[19] Ibid.

[20] Cell Leader Intern Training, (Singapore: Touch Ministries International, 1996), Section 5, p. 4.

[21] Floyd L. Schwanz, *Growing Small Groups* (Kansas City, MI: Beacon Hill Press, 1995), p. 140.

[22] To order these prayer profiles, contact: The Unreached People Project, 13855 Plank Road, Baker, LA 70714 USA, Phone: 504-774-2002, Email: upg@bethany-wpc.org.

[23] C. Peter Wagner, *Churches That Pray* (Ventura, CA: Regal Books, 1993), p. 119.

[24] Jeffrey Arnold, *The Big Book on Small Groups* (Downers Grove, IL: Inter Varsity Press, 1992), p. 170.

[25] Ralph Neighbour Jr. "Barriers to Growth," *Cell Church* magazine (Summer 1997), p. 16.

CHAPTER 5

[1] C. Kirk Hadaway, *Church Growth Principles: Separating Fact from Fiction* (Nashville, TN: Broadman Press, 1991), pp. 120-121.

[2] Ted W. Engstrom, *The Making of a Christian Leader* (Grand Rapids, MI: Zondervan Publishing House, 1976), p. 106.

[3] William Carey is often referred to as the "father of the modern missionary movement." Carey delivered this quote as part of a sermon on Isaiah 54:2.

[4] David Yonggi Cho, *Successful Home Cell Groups*. (Miami, FL: Logos International 1981), p. 162.

[5] David Yonggi Cho, *Church Growth*. Manual No. 7. (Seoul, Korea: Church Growth International, 1995) p. 18

[6] Ibid, p. 18.

[7] Galloway, *The Small Group Book* (Grand Rapids, MI: Fleming H. Revell, 1995), p. 62.

[8] C. Kirk Hadaway, Stuart A. Wright, and Francis DuBose, *Home Cell Groups and House Churches*. (Nashville, TN: Broadman Press, 1987), p. 101.

[9] George Barna, *The Power of Vision* (Ventura, CA: Regal Books, 1992), p. 29.

[10] Warren Bennis and Burt Nanus, *Leaders: The Strategies For Taking Charge* (New York: Harper Perennial, 1985), p. 107.

[11] Raymond E. Ebbett, a C&MA missionary and cell-church planter in Spain, mentions this story in C&MA CELLNET #04B, Fri. 6/20/97.

[12] C. Kirk Hadaway, Stuart A. Wright, and Francis DuBose, *Home Cell Groups and House Churches*. (Nashville, TN: Broadman Press, 1987), p. 19.

[13] Karen Hurston, "The Importance of Small Group Multiplication" in *Global Church Growth* (Vol. XXXII, no 4, 1995) p. 12.

[14] George Barna, *The Power of Vision* (Ventura, CA: Regal Books, 1992), p. 148.

[15] Quoted in C. Peter Wagner, "Pragmatic Strategy for Tomorrow's Mission" in *God Man and Church Growth* (Grand Rapids, MI: Baker Book House, 1973), pp. 146,147.

[16] Warren Bennis and Burt Nanus, *Leaders: The Strategies For Taking Charge* (New York: Harper Perennial, 1985), p. 226.

[17] Richard B. Wilke, *And Are We Yet Alive?* (Nashville, TN: Abingdon Press, 1986), p. 59.

[18] J. Peters Thomas, *Thriving on Chaos* (New York: Harper Perennial, 1987), p. 284.

[19] Ibid.

[20] In Cho's church, the goal is for each cell group to win one family to Christ every six months. If the group does not accomplish that goal, Cho send them to Yoido's Prayer Mountain.

[21] Ralph Neighbour, *New Believer's Station* (Houston, TX: Touch Publications, 1995), p. 75.

CHAPTER 6

[1] Matthew Henry, <u>Matthew Henry's Commentary on the Bible</u> (Peabody, MA: Hendrickson Publishers, 1991), on CD ROM. Commentary on John 4:27-42.

[2] Larry Kreider referred to this conversation with Cho during a panel discussion at the Post Denominational seminar on May 22, 1996.

[3] Carl George, *The Coming Church Revolution* (Grand Rapids, MI: Fleming H. Revell, 1994), p. 48.

[4] Roland Allen, *Missionary Methods: St. Paul's or Ours?* (Grand Rapids: Eerdmans, 1962), pp. 84-94.

[5] Roland Allen, *The Spontaneous Expansion of the Church and the Causes Which Hinder It.* 3rd Ed. (London: World Dominion Press, 1956), p. 9.

[6] David Sheppard, *Built as a City: God and the Urban World Today* (London: Hodder and Stoughton Publishers, 1974), p. 123.

[7] Aubrey Malphurs, *Planting Growing Churches for the 21st Century.* Grand Rapids, MI: Baker Book House, 1992, pp. 145-146.

[8] C. Kirk Hadaway, Stuart A. Wright, and Francis DuBose, *Home Cell Groups and House Churches.* (Nashville, TN: Broadman Press, 1987), p. 203.

[9] Eddie Gibbs quotes Wasdell as coining the term "leader breeder" to describe leadership development in cell groups, in *I Believe in Church Growth* (Grand Rapids: Eerdmans Publishing Company, 1981), p. 260.

[10] C. Kirk Hadaway, Stuart A. Wright, and Francis DuBose, *Home Cell Groups and House Churches.* (Nashville, TN: Broadman Press, 1987), p. 201.

[11] *Journey Guide* and other valuable cell leader tools are available from TOUCH Outreach Ministries. For more information visit their website (www.touchusa.org) or call 800-735-5865. (Outside the United States: 281-497-7901.)

[12] Ralph Neighbour Jr., *The Shepherd's Guidebook: A Leader's Guide for the Cell Group Church* (Houston, TX: Touch Publications, 1992), p. 42.

[13] Faith Community Baptist Church in Singapore trains cell leaders to baptize and serve communion in the cell, but leaders did not serve communion in the cell in the other case-study churches.

[14] Carl George, *Prepare Your Church for the Future* (Grand Rapids, MI: Fleming H. Revell, 1992), p. 68.

[15] These are the leadership characteristics listed by Larry Kreider in *House to House* (Houston, TX: Touch Publications, 1995), pp. 41-53.

[16] Karen Hurston, *Growing the World's Largest Church* (Springfield, MI: Chrism, 1994), p. 68.

[17] Hurston, p. 194.

[18] Dale Galloway, *The Small Group Book* (Grand Rapids, MI: Fleming H. Revell), p. 105.

[19] Quoted in Carl George, *Prepare Your Church for the Future* (Grand Rapids, MI: Fleming H. Revell, 1992), pp. 203-204.

[20] The amount of training at the time of the survey varied greatly from church to church. Living Water in Lima, Peru, required a one-year training course; The International Charismatic Mission required a weekend retreat and a three-month core course; Elim required a four-week leadership training course; the leadership training at Faith Community Baptist Church was more extensive.

[21] The head pastor of a C&MA church in Colombia used a manual that recommends holding bimonthly training sessions with all cell leadership. In my 3-1/2 years of missionary work in Ecuador, these bimonthly training sessions proved to be the backbone of the cell ministry.

[22] In his book *Where Do We Go From Here?* (Houston, TX: Touch Publications, 1990, pp. 73-80,) Ralph Neighbour Jr. talks about the apprentice system (or Jethro model) that is so common in cell churches today.

[23] The main books used for leader training are *El Lider En Los Grupos (Group Leaders C.A.F.E. 2000)*, and a book written by César Castellanos (1996) called *Encuentro* (Encounter).

[24] At ICM, it is common knowledge that its young people's ministry is the most effective in the church. Leaders there say that ideas and methods are tested among the young people; if they work, they then are implemented in the entire church.

[25] There is a growing movement toward cell planting, which places a high emphasis on individual evangelism and multiplication. Team ministry is also a part of cell planting through the discipleship process ("Groups of Twelve").

[26] At times the administration might have a meeting for all the treasurers to share about a pressing financial need in the church. All of the money received in the group goes directly to the church, with the exception of those groups that contract buses for the Saturday service. In that case, every other offering is for the church. Treasurers are entrusted to take the tithes and offerings of the people.

[27] Warren Bennis and Burt Nanus, *Leaders: The Strategies for Taking Charge* (New York: Harper Perennial, 1985), p. 71.

[28] Quoted in Thomas J. Peters, *Thriving on Chaos* (New York: Harper Perennial, 1987), p. 315.

[29] Ibid., pp. 316-317.

CHAPTER 7

[1] The most common interpretation of "new people" refers to those who have visited the cell group or the church but are not yet committed as members.

[2] Larry Stockstill, "'Calling Out to Win the Lost:' An Interview with Larry Stockstill," *Ministries Today* (July/August, 1996), pp. 37-40.

[3] Herb Miller, *How to Build a Magnetic Church.* Creative Leadership Series. Lyle Schaller, ed. (Nashville, TN: Abingdon Press, 1987), pp. 72-73.

[4] Galloway, *The Small Group Book* (Grand Rapids, MI: Fleming H. Revell, 1995), p. 62.

[5] Miller, p. 32.

[6] Richard Price and Pat Springer, *Rapha's Handbook for Group Leaders* (Houston, TX: Rapha Publishing, 1991), p. 132.

[7] Ralph Neighbour Jr., *The Shepherd's Guidebook: A Leader's Guide for the Cell Group Church* (Houston, TX: Touch Publications, 1992), p. 61

[8] Ralph Neighbour Jr., *Building Awareness Opening Hearts* (Houston, TX: Touch Publications, 1992), p.72.

[9] David Yonggi Cho, *Church Growth.* Manual No. 7. (Seoul, Korea: Church Growth International, 1995) p. 19

CHAPTER 8

[1] Dale Galloway, *The Small Group Book* (Grand Rapids, MI: Fleming H. Revell, 1995), p. 122.

[2] David Yonggi Cho, *Recruiting Staff For a Large Church.* Church Growth Lectures. Audio tape 2. Fuller Theological Seminar, School of World Mission. Pasadena, CA, 1984.

[3] Michael C. Mack, *The Synergy Church* (Grand Rapids, MI: Baker Book House, 1996), p.53.

[4] A quotation from Larry Stockstill's handout from the Post-Denominational Seminar (May 22, 1996).

[5] The number 700,000 is a membership figure of people who tithe to Yoido Full Gospel Church and thus are on the roll. Sunday morning attendance does not come close to 700,000. One Sunday in April 1997, about 153,000 people attended Yoido's seven services. About 100,000 more attended one of the 12 regional chapels throughout Seoul, Korea.

[6] Karen Hurston, *Growing the World's Largest Church* (Springfield, MI: Chrism, 1994), p. 107.

[7] Paul Meier, Gene A. Getz, Richard A. Meier, and Allen R. Doran, *Filling the Holes in Our Souls: Caring Groups that Build Lasting Relationship* (Chicago: Moody Press, 1992), p.180.

[8]Peter Wagner, ed., *Church Growth: The State of the Art* (Wheaton, IL: Tyndale, 1986), pp. 74-84.

[9]Dale Galloway, *20/20 Vision* (Portland, OR: Scott Publishing, 1986), p. 144.

[10]Peggy Kannaday, ed. *Church Growth and the Home Cell System* (Seoul, Korea: Church Growth International, 1995), p.19.

[11]*Small Group Evangelism* (Pasadena, CA: Fuller Theological Seminary, 1996).

[12]Peace, p.36.

[13]Peace, p. 27.

[14]Howard A. Snyder, *The Radical Wesley and Patterns for Church Renewal* (Downers Grove, IL: Inter Varsity Press, 1980), p. 55.

[15]David Sheppard, Built *As A City: God and the Urban World Today* (London: Hodder and Stoughton Publishers, 1974), p. 127.

[16]David Hocking, *The Seven Laws of Christian Leadership* (Ventura, CA: Regal Books, 1991), p.63.

[17]Stephen Covey, *The 7 Habits of Highly Effective People* (New York: Simon & Schuster, 1989), p. 239.

[18]Judy Hamlin, *The Small Group Leaders Training Course* (Colorado Springs, CO: Navpress, 1990), pp. 54-57.

[19]The two E's (evangelism and edification) or the two M's (ministry and mission) provide easy memory guides. First, cells minister to one another and cells must multiply by reaching out.

[20]Four booklets of the Track Pack (Houston, TX: Touch Publications, 1996) focus on teaching the new believer to reach out to non-Christians. Also in *The Shepherd's Guidebook: A Leader's Guide for the Cell Group Church* (Houston, TX: Touch Publications, 1992), p. 27, Ralph Neighbour Jr. deals with the different classes of believers.

[21]Ralph Neighbour Jr., *Building Groups Opening Hearts* (Houston: Touch Publications, 1991), p. 60.

CHAPTER 9

[1]F.F. Bruce, The Epistles to the Ephesians and Colossians in *The New International Commentary in the New Testament* (Grand Rapids: Eerdmans, 1957), pp. 309-310.

[2]David Yonggi Cho, *Successful Home Cell Groups.* (Miami, FL: Logos International 1981), p. 59.

[3]Carl George, *The Coming Church Revolution* (Grand Rapids, MI: Fleming H. Revell, 1994), p. 94.

[4]Ron Nichols, *Good Things Come in Small Groups* (Downers Grove, IL: Inter Varsity Press, 1985), p. 25.

[5]George G. Hunter III, *Church for the Unchurched* (Nashville, TN: Abingdon Press, 1996), pp. 116-117.

[6]Ronald J. Sider, *Rich Christians in an Age of Hunger* (Downers Grove, IL: Inter Varsity Press, 1984), p. 187.

[7]Ibid, 185.

[8]The Touch Community Service Center is a separate, non-profit organization that receives financial assistance from the Singapore government. For this reason, open proclamation of the gospel is not permitted. Most, not all, of the staff members belong to the church.

[9]Judy Johnson, *Good Things Come in Small Groups* (Downers Grove, IL: Inter Varsity Press, 1985), p. 176.

CHAPTER 10

[1]Schwanz, p. 144

[2]Ralph Neighbour, *Where Do We Go From Here?* (Houston, TX: Touch Publications, 1990), p. 70.

[3]In David Cho's *Successful Home Cell Groups* (Miami, FL: Logos International 1981), Chapter 13 discusses the importance of recognizing cell leadership before the congregation.

[4]Dale Galloway, *The Small Group Book* (Grand Rapids, MI: Fleming H. Revell 1995), p. 126.

[5] John K. Brilhart, *Effective Group Discussion* 4th ed. (Dubuque, Iowa: Wm. C. Brown Company Publishers, 1982), p. 59.

[6] Dale Galloway, *The Small Group Book* (Grand Rapids, MI: Fleming H. Revell, 1995), p. 145.

[7] John Mallison, *Growing Christians in Small Groups* (London: Scripture Union, 1989), p. 25.

[8] Carl George, *How To Break Growth Barriers* (Grand Rapids, MI: Baker Book House, 1993), p. 136.

[9] Donald McGavran, *Understanding Church Growth*. 3rd edition (Grand Rapids, MI: William B. Eerdmans Publishing Company, 1990), pp. 215-216, 223.

[10] Karen Hurston, *Growing the World's Largest Church* (Springfield, MI: Chrism, 1994), p. 93.

[11] Robert E. Logan, *Beyond Church Growth* (Grand Rapids, MI: Fleming H. Revell, 1989), p. 138.

[12] Bob Logan and Jeannette Buller offer excellent insight about cell multiplication in a computer diskette called CompuCoach 96. This program for Windows and Apple systems focuses on church planting.

[13] Ralph Neighbour, *The Shepherd's Guidebook: A Leader's Guide for the Cell Group Church* (Houston, TX: Touch Publications, 1992), pp. 32-35.

[14] Ibid, p. 113.

[15] Floyd L. Schwanz, *Growing Small Groups* (Kansas City, MI: Beacon Hill Press, 1995), p. 145.

[16] FCBC Trainees Manual, Section 6, p. 3.

[17] Carl George, *Prepare Your Church for the Future* (Grand Rapids, MI: Fleming H. Revell, 1992), p. 101.

CHAPTER 11

[1] Ibid, p. 44.

[2] At least half of the leadership staff are women. Claudia Castellanos has modeled a strong leadership influence. She formed part of the Colombia senate in 1989.

[3] The new thrust in March 1997 was for each discipler of 12 also to maintain an evangelistic cell group.

[4] The young people's cell groups are a separate category. They organize their own statistics and program.

[5] One of Pierson's areas of expertise is in the spiritual movements that have impacted the history of mission.

[6] The departments include: young people, professionals, worship, spiritual warfare, men's ministry, women's ministry, counseling, ushers, counseling, follow-up, social action, pastoral care, accounting, video, sound, bookstore, etc.

[7] A ministerial department such as sound, social action, or accounting has fewer cells than the larger ministries such as young people, worship, men's ministry or women's ministry. But the leaders of these smaller ministries have 12 disciples who in turn have cell groups.

[8] In October 1996, the larger departments holding their weekly congregational meetings in the sanctuary were: Men, Spiritual Warfare, Healing and Miracles, Worship, Couples, Women, and Young People. Adolescents and small children have their own cells. In October 1996, the junior high department had 171 cell groups. They also had their congregational meeting and met again on Sunday morning. The cell groups for children might be best described as home Bible clubs led by adults. But the goal is to encourage the children to make their own disciples and to take more responsibility in leading the group. The children also have their own congregational meeting during the week.

[9] Normally, between 20 and 500 people respond to the invitation.

[10] When I visited ICM in March 1997, nine Encounters were scheduled for one weekend with approximately 500 young people attending.

[11] Larry's quote in *Ministries Today* (July, 1996, 39). Those "saved" is one category in the required weekly cell report forms.

[12] Neighbour, *Building*, pp. 72-73.

[13] Neighbour, *Building*, p. 73.

[14] As of July 1997, Bethany was having trouble receiving the weekly statistical reports from the new homogenous cell groups.

[15] More recently, he gathers all of the cell leaders together on a monthly basis instead of a weekly basis. According to Pastor Larry, supervision is just that super-vision. Each month, he tries to pump up leaders with an understanding of the importance of their role.

[16] Larry Stockstill, "'Celling Out' to Win the Lost." An Interview with Larry Stockstill, *Ministries Today* magazine (July/August, 1996), pp. 37.

[17] Pastor Larry made these comments during his senior pastor's luncheon at the June 1996 cell conference. However, these requirements have not been "fleshed out."

[18] This statistic was in the Church Visitor's Guide (June, 1996), p. 16

CHAPTER 12

[1] If a targeted area cannot easily be reached by multiplying a group, Elim is finding that it is often better to look for someone in that area to open their home for a cell plant and then provide a trained leader to start a new group.

[2] Elim had not been influenced by outside missionaries. Nor was Pastor Sergio Solórzano trained in the United States or Europe.

[3] Some years, the focus is on nurturing cells as opposed to multiplying them and, thus, no groups multiply.

[4] When new cells are planted, frequently no existing group takes responsibility for the new group.

[5] The mother cell's leadership team makes a large commitment: two cells a week for three months. So the leadership team is encouraged to meet on a rotating basis. For example, if there are five members on the leadership team, perhaps three will attend one Tuesday and the other two the next Tuesday.

[6] A strict order for these counseling/assessment times is laid out in LAC's cell manual.

[7] The director of the cell groups says that he might allow a group to start with a combination of leader and assistant or leader and treasurer. However, a new group needs at least three members before beginning.

[8] Because of the in-depth process of leadership preparation, only one of every 10 cell groups fails.

[9] For the first three months, the new groups follow specific material called "The Victorious Christian Life." These lessons cover topics designed to teach faith, obedience, confession, trials, prayer, and the Word of God.

[10] This evangelism takes several forms. The entire zone might plan an evangelistic activity (e.g., movie, special speaker). The cell group might reach out to the neighborhood through some special type of outreach (e.g., invitation to Mother's Day celebration or a special dinner). These special group events do not occur on Wednesday, when the group must follow the normal cell group format.

[11] For example, Dixie Rosales is director of the entire cell ministry at LAC in Tegucigalpa. He started as a cell member 1986, soon became assistant cell leader, and then was asked to lead a new cell. That new cell eventually gave birth to four new groups. Dixie then was asked to be a zone pastor over 25 cell groups. Because of his success there, he now directs the entire cell ministry.

[12] Larry Kreider, *House to House* (Houston, TX: Touch Publications), p.7.

[13] Larry is talking about both rapid cell multiplication and church multiplication (i.e., church planting). He made this statement on May 22 during the Post-Denominational seminar.

[14] This goal is very high. At this point there are some 530 cells in the church.

[15] Jim Egli, *North Star Strategies* Special Report #5, (Urbana, Illinois, 1993), p. 12

INDEX